PULL UP A CHAIR
You, Me, and the Gospel of John

Lorie Looney Keene

NEW HOPE
P U B L I S H E R S
Birmingham, Alabama

New Hope® Publishers
P. O. Box 12065
Birmingham, AL 35202-2065
www.newhopepublishers.com

New Hope Publishers is a division of WMU®.

Library of Congress Cataloging-in-Publication Data

Keene, Lorie Looney, 1977-
  Pull up a chair : you, me, and the Gospel of John / Lorie Looney Keene.
     p. cm.
  ISBN 978-1-59669-202-2 (sc)
  1. Bible. N.T. John--Commentaries. 2. Christian women--Religious life. I. Title.
  BS2615.53.K43 2008
  226.5'07--dc22
                          2007050440

ISBN-10: 1-59669-202-2
ISBN-13: 978-1-59669-202-2

N084130 • 0508 • 4M1

Dedication

This study is dedicated to several special people in my life:

My parents, Gary and Debra Looney,
who, through their love and examples,
demonstrate to me what it means
to know and walk with the Lord

My sister, Rachel,
who has tolerated my endless talking
and teaching all of her life

And especially, my husband, Stephen,
who remains my hero
both in life and in the faith

Table of Contents

Introduction

As women, we love to chat, socialize, and share stories. This study is designed to encourage women to do these things, through pulling up a chair weekly for a time of discussion, introspection, and fellowshipping over the Gospel of John. *Pull Up a Chair* is not intended to be an exhaustive study of the Gospel of John but rather an overall look at the main topics and themes John reveals in each chapter.

Instructions for This Study

Each week, read through one chapter of John and work through the associated week's study, answering the questions. Meet weekly with other study participants for a time of review, discussion, and, of course, fellowship! Remember to begin each meeting with prayer, stay committed to what the Scriptures teach, and keep the gospel at the center of your conversation at all times. Continually point toward the Cross those who have not yet come to know Christ, and always refer back to the Cross those who have already placed their faith in Him.

Why This Book?

I have chosen to write a study through the Book of John primarily because, in my opinion, this is one of the most remarkable sources in which we can fully examine the life and purpose of Jesus Christ. The Scriptures inform us that unless a person has a personal relationship with Jesus, he or she cannot have a relationship with God the Father (John 3:17–18). If the choice between eternal condemnation and an eternal relationship with a Holy God lies in one's understanding of God's Son, Jesus, then knowing more about Him is extremely important.

Everyone has an opinion about Jesus Christ. Rather than basing our opinions on what others say about Him, why not let Him speak for Himself? The Book of John clearly walks us through the life of Jesus Christ, as He boldly makes claims about His identity. Room for confusion is removed when we allow the actual words of Jesus to speak louder than the opinions of others.

Background on the Book of John

The Book of John is one of the four books known as the Gospels: Matthew, Mark, Luke, and John. The Gospels are grouped at the beginning of the New Testament. The word *gospel* is translated from a Greek term meaning "good news." The four Gospels each proclaim the good news of Christ from four individual perspectives. Each book is also named after its author.

The author of John is often called *the beloved disciple*, denoting the special relationship he had with Jesus Christ. John referred to himself as the disciple Jesus loved in his descriptions of the times he fellowshipped with Jesus and the other disciples at Jesus's last supper, stood at the foot of Jesus Christ while He was on the Cross, received news from Mary Magdalene about Jesus's body being missing, recognized the resurrected Lord on the shore of the sea, and followed Jesus and Peter as Peter received his restoration assignment (John 13:23; 19:26; 20:2; 21:7; 21:20). John lived with Christ, ate with Christ, saw Him die on the Cross, and ultimately witnessed evidence of the glorious Resurrection. This firsthand account provides a multitude of illuminations into the person of Christ.

The beginning of John 1 reads a little like the first verse in Genesis, starting off *"In the beginning."* John immediately directs the reader to the ultimate supremacy and eternity of the Word, who plays out in John 1 to be Jesus Christ Himself. Readers are instantly challenged to view Christ not merely as a temporal human being, but rather as a spiritual being who has existed alongside God the Father from the beginning of time. John then introduces the reader to Jesus, the Christ, as an adult rather than starting with Jesus's birth, as do Matthew and Luke.

Through the entire book, the reader is invited into the life, ministry, and ultimate destiny of Christ. The claims of Christ are made clear through this book: for example, He is God (John 1:1–3), He is the Son of God (John 1:34; 20:31), you must know Jesus Christ to know God (John 14:6), and you must have a believing relationship with Jesus Christ, the Son of God, to have eternal life with God (John 3:16–18).

Inspired Word of God

The premise of this study is the foundational trust that the Scriptures are the inspired Word of God, written by men who were divinely led by God. As a result of this belief, every word contained in the Scriptures is therefore accepted as truth. This truth is the measure to which we are called to compare our lives.

Note to Fellow Sojourners Through the Book of John

I am so excited to be sharing with you this incredible story of my Lord. As we walk together through the Scriptures, you will either be reminded or see for the first time that God the Father loves you and desires for you to both know Him and have a personal relationship with Him through His Son, Jesus Christ. If you already have a relationship with Christ, my prayer is that this study will both strengthen your walk and encourage you to share His truth with others. If you currently do not know Christ, my prayer is that you will allow the words of these Scriptures to open your heart and mind to His truth. You are loved with an everlasting love. You were created to know and walk with Christ. You are invaluable to the Father. Know Him. Love Him. Walk with Him. Share Him.

I am already praying for you.

The Word in the World

Plant the Seed

As encouragement for each of us to share God's Word and Way with others, examples of sharing and applicable Scriptures are provided on The Word in the World pages.

> *"The sower went out to sow his seed; and as he sowed, some fell beside the road, and it was trampled under foot and the birds of the air ate it up. Other seed fell on rocky soil, and as soon as it grew up, it withered away, because it had no moisture. Other seed fell among the thorns; and the thorns grew up with it and choked it out. Other seed fell into the good soil, and grew up, and produced a crop a hundred times as great." As He said these things, He would call out, "He who has ears to hear, let him hear." ... "Now the parable is this: the seed is the word of God."*
> —Luke 8:5–8, 11

When we share God's Word and our faith in Jesus Christ, we are planting seed. We may not see the results of our sharing, but we must be faithful in planting the seed. Without seed, there is no harvest. So start planting!

In the Beginning Was the Word

People Introduced

The Word (Jesus Christ)

John the Baptist (the cousin of Jesus Christ; predestined by God to announce the arrival of Christ)

Andrew (brother of Simon Peter; fisherman; first a disciple [follower] of John the Baptist; became a disciple of Jesus Christ)

Simon Peter (brother of Andrew; fisherman; became a disciple of Jesus Christ)

Philip (became a disciple of Jesus Christ)

Nathanael (probably became a disciple of Jesus Christ; most likely the disciple called Bartholomew by other Gospel writers)

> *And the Word became flesh, and dwelt among us, and we saw His glory, glory as of the only begotten from the Father, full of grace and truth. John testified about Him and cried out, saying, "This was He of whom I said, 'He who comes after me has a higher rank than I, for He existed before me.'"*
> —John 1:14–15

John 1:1–28

The first chapter of John introduces us to the Word and briefly to John the Baptist.

The Word has been *with* God and *was* God from the beginning (John 1:1–2). You see, God reveals Himself to man in three persons: the Father, the Son (Jesus Christ), and the Holy Spirit. This concept is very important. So where does the Word fit in? John 1:14 states, *"And the Word became flesh, and dwelt among us, and we saw His glory, glory as of the only begotten from the Father, full of grace and truth."* The Word actually turns out to be God the Son, Jesus Christ—Jesus Christ is the Word. That being the case, in these first few verses, we are told that Christ has existed from all eternity and shares in the very essence of God! He is God and has all the qualities of God.

 Discuss some of the qualities of God. (For example, He is holy, sovereign, perfect, and timeless.)

All of the qualities of God are encompassed by the personhood of Jesus Christ! Just as God is holy, Christ, too, is holy. Think about it: If God is perfect and Christ has been with God the Father since the beginning, and has all this time been God, then He, too, must be perfect. All parts or aspects of a pure, perfect source must also be pure. God is the source of truth (John 17:17; 1 John 5:20). Since Christ is God, He, too, is 100 percent truth (John 14:6). This purity of truth is impossible to find in any other earthly existence. Consider with me your relationships. Parents, friends, and co-workers may possess a lot of truth in them. For example, your best friend may tell you the truth 99 percent of the time. However, even she occasionally lies or makes a mistake; after all, she is human. Christ, however, cannot lie. He must be 100 percent truth, because He is God.

 How does the understanding that Christ is 100 percent true and trustworthy, carrying within Him the essence of God, cause you to consider the words He has spoken?

> *In the beginning was the Word, and the Word was with God, and the Word was God. He was in the beginning with God. All things were created through Him, and apart from Him not one thing was created that has been created.*
> —John 1:1–3 (HCSB)

All things were created through Christ (v. 3). The source of life has always existed in Him, and that life is described as *"the Light of men"* (v. 4). Only through Christ can all things be made clear. If you feel as though you are stumbling through life without a relationship with Christ, it is because you are! We were not created to live and navigate through life apart from Him.

Christ came into the world, yet the world did not recognize Him (v. 10). I have often heard people say, "I could believe in Christ too if only I had the chance to see Him." Verse 10 shows the fallacy of that statement: *"He was in the world, and the world was made through Him, and the world did not know Him."* Christ came into the world and met people face-to-face, yet He was not received by most. However, despite mass disbelief, Christ administers an amazing promise to all persons who *do* believe in Him.

> *But as many as received Him, to them He gave the right to become children of God, even to those who believe in His name.*
> —John 1:12

 According to the promise in John 1:12, what does Christ give to those who believe in Him?

"The right to become children of God" is directly related to our belief in the name (or person) of Jesus Christ. This destroys the false belief that salvation can be obtained through anything other than a personal relationship with Jesus Christ.

Because of the sin of mankind (Romans 3:23) and the desperate state of hopelessness sin brings (Romans 6:23), God sent His Son into the world so that through belief in His Son, we might receive eternal life (John 3:16). Romans 10:9 states that salvation occurs through our *confession* that Jesus is Lord and our *belief* that God has raised Him from the dead. There are no second choices, no other options, no "exit number 2's," found on the road from sin toward eternal life with God. Thus, it is imperative that we begin immediately to understand our own view of who Jesus Christ is and where our faith actually lies. Do we depend on our own qualifications and abilities or on His unfailing love and perfect sacrifice?

> *For all have sinned and fall short of the glory of God.*
> —Romans 3:23

> *For the wages of sin is death, but the free gift of God is eternal life in Christ Jesus our Lord.*
> —Romans 6:23

"For God so loved the world, that He gave His only begotten Son, that whoever believes in Him shall not perish, but have eternal life."
—John 3:16

That if you confess with your mouth Jesus as Lord, and believe in your heart that God raised Him from the dead, you will be saved; for with the heart a person believes, resulting in righteousness, and with the mouth he confesses, resulting in salvation.
—Romans 10:9–10

 Read John 1:6–9, 14–15. What was John the Baptist's role?

There came a man sent from God, whose name was John. He came as a witness, to testify about the Light, so that all might believe through him. He was not the Light, but he came to testify about the Light. There was the true Light which, coming into the world, enlightens every man....

And the Word became flesh, and dwelt among us, and we saw His glory, glory as of the only begotten from the Father, full of grace and truth. John testified about Him and cried out, saying, "This was He of whom I said, 'He who comes after me has a higher rank than I, for He existed before me.'"
—John 1:6–9, 14–15

Scriptures tell us that the John discussed in these verses, John the Baptist, had a very specific role: the announcer of the news of Jesus Christ. He was sent by God to be a witness about the coming of Christ. He was not Christ, but rather the forerunner to His appearing. I picture John's role as a herald of the coming King. In history, great kings and royalty have been known to send people ahead of them to wave banners, shout, play trumpets, and create a stir among people in order to prepare them for the arrival of someone "great." At a much more significant level, this was John the Baptist's job.

Unlike guardsmen or royal officers who often wore badges or recognizable markings to identify them, John the Baptist had only his testimony. Therefore, it was not unusual for John to have to explain himself. When approached by Jewish officials, John was quick to state that he was *not* the Messiah. I appreciate his instant honesty. Think about it, John was gaining attention from his message—so much attention that even the Jewish officials were curious as to who this man was. He could easily have been tempted to take some credit for himself, but instead, John, pulling his identity from the prophecy of Isaiah (40:3), simply referred to himself as *"A VOICE OF ONE CRYING IN THE WILDERNESS, 'MAKE STRAIGHT THE WAY OF THE LORD'"* (John 1:23).

John 1:29–42

John the Baptist earned his name in history because of his occupation as one who baptized. Scriptures show us that John paved the way for the coming of Christ by announcing His imminent arrival and baptizing in water those who believed his message. In John 1:29–42, we are given a glimpse into John's first moments with the One whom he had been announcing. Once again, John did not waste words or time. The moment John saw Jesus Christ approaching, he made this proclamation: *"Behold, the Lamb of God who takes away the sin of the world! This is He on behalf of whom I said, 'After me comes a Man who has a higher rank than I, for He existed before me'"* (John 1:29–30).

Explain how John 1:30 relates to what you have already learned in John 1:1–3.

This confession of John demonstrates his understanding that Christ, though wearing the flesh of man and called by the name *Jesus,* has existed from all eternity! Though *"the Word became flesh, and dwelt among us"* (John 1:14), the One who was born on this earth as Jesus is none other than the eternal Son of God. Therefore, John was able to say, *"He existed before me"* (v. 30). Although John had not previously met Jesus face-to-face, God had promised him a sign.

Read John 1:32–34, and describe the sign God promised John—the sign that would identify Christ.

John testified saying, "I have seen the Spirit descending as a dove out of heaven, and He remained upon Him. I did not recognize Him, but He who sent me to baptize in water said to me, 'He upon whom you see the Spirit descending and remaining upon Him, this is the

One who baptizes in the Holy Spirit.' I myself have seen, and have testified that this is the Son of God."
—John 1:32–34

Upon recognizing the sign God had promised, John announced another title for Jesus Christ: *"Son of God."* There is no mistaking John's intention for his followers to understand Christ as deity. John had so well taught his followers to be looking forward to Christ's arrival that upon His appearance the next day, two of John's disciples left him and began following Jesus Christ. What an amazing testimony of John's intention and discipleship! Rather than getting jealous for the attention of his followers, John rejoiced to see them turn from him (the messenger) toward Christ (John 3:27–30).

 According to John 1:35–39, what was the length of time between John's disciples noticing Christ and their decision to follow Him?

Again the next day John was standing with two of his disciples, and he looked at Jesus as He walked, and said, "Behold, the Lamb of God!" The two disciples heard him speak, and they followed Jesus. And Jesus turned and saw them following, and said to them, "What do you seek?" They said to Him, "Rabbi (which translated means Teacher), where are You staying?" He said to them, "Come, and you will see." So they came and saw where He was staying; and they stayed with Him that day, for it was about the tenth hour.
—John 1:35–39

They followed Christ that very day! This is where we first meet Andrew and Simon Peter. Andrew heard the good news about Jesus being the Lamb of God and followed Him immediately. Then he did something very important: he shared the truth about Jesus being the Messiah with his brother Simon. Andrew was so convinced that this Jesus was, indeed, the Christ, the long-awaited Savior, that he found his brother and said, *"We have found the Messiah"* (John 1:41). When Simon was brought to Jesus, Jesus gave him the name *Cephas*, or the modern name *Peter*, which means "Rock."

John 1:43–51

In these verses we meet Philip and Nathanael. Unlike some who want to see signs from heaven or to experience a huge miraculous event before surrendering their lives to Christ, Philip responded to two simple words: *"Follow Me"* (John 1:43). The words may be ordinary, but the One who spoke them is anything but ordinary.

 What pattern do you see when you compare Andrew's and Philip's faith? (Compare John 1:40–42 and John 1:45–46.)

One of the two who heard John speak and followed Him, was Andrew, Simon Peter's brother. He found first his own brother Simon and said to him, "We have found the Messiah" (which translated means Christ). He brought him to Jesus. Jesus looked at him and said, "You are Simon the son of John; you shall be called Cephas" (which is translated Peter).
—John 1:40–42

Philip found Nathanael and said to him, "We have found Him of whom Moses in the Law and also the Prophets wrote—Jesus of Nazareth, the son of Joseph." Nathanael said to him, "Can any good thing come out of Nazareth?" Philip said to him, "Come and see."
—John 1:45–46

The Scriptures do not give record of people coming to faith in Christ and then desiring to run and hide from all family and friends. The accounts are quite the opposite. We see new believers having the zeal and courage to step out and share with those around them. Such was the case with both Andrew and Philip. Both of these men, upon deciding to follow Christ, immediately found another person and shared their newfound faith.

Some individuals, like Nathanael, were given remarkable signs to encourage their coming to faith. While walking toward Christ, Nathanael was greeted with the remark, *"Behold, an Israelite indeed, in whom there is no deceit!"* (John 1:47). Demonstrating his weakly sprouting faith, Nathanael asked, *"How do You know me?"* (v. 48). Christ replied by sharing something no one else could have known.

How did Jesus Christ respond to Nathanael in John 1:48?

To ease Nathanael's doubt, Christ told him exactly where he had last been! To this comment, Nathanael instantly proclaimed this: *"You are the Son of God; You are the King of Israel"* (John 1:49). Sounds great for a moment, doesn't it? Many of us would love for God to show us a sign or whisper something only He could know in our ears, just to assure us that He is real and really here with us. This, however, is not the kind of faith we are encouraged to seek. Although Christ promised Nathanael that he would see greater things than this in his lifetime (v. 50), faith is what Christ desires and honors most, rather than belief by sight (John 20:29).

Personal Reflection

(These questions are intended for personal reflection, personal application, and discussion. Spend unhurried time meditating on these questions in light of what you learned from God's Word during this week's study, and allow the Word to take root and bring forth fruit in your life.)

1. **In what ways has this chapter in John challenged or strengthened my faith in Jesus Christ?**

2. **Have I ever personally placed my faith in Jesus Christ as my Savior and Lord? If I have not, what is currently keeping me from doing so? If I have, how is my faith in Christ affecting my daily life in regard to this lesson?**

The Word in the World

Melissa: Meet the Need First

Late one evening, I went to a local superstore and bought a headset to motivate me to get up and start walking in the mornings. Feeling the conviction of the headset lying on my bedside table, I arose the next morning and went walking on and around campus.

The weather was great. I spent the first part of the walk with the headset off, just talking with the Lord. I had been trying to be more consistent in asking Him to make me aware of how and where He was working around me. Well, the answer to my request that particular day came about 15 minutes into my walk!

As I rounded a corner, returning to the campus, I noticed a young girl driving up to me in a car, rolling down her window. She looked a little frazzled and asked if I knew of any place to use the Internet for free. She explained that she just found out her friend may have been killed in a car wreck, and that she needed to look it up on the Internet. Nothing was open yet. At that moment, the Lord reminded me of what I had just prayed.

In the assurance that I was being invited to participate with the Lord in His work, I followed His prompting. And the next thing I knew, she and I were driving toward my apartment. She used my computer to look up the information she needed. I discovered that she was newly married and new to Louisville. I am sure you can guess what I asked next. No, she did not have a church home yet. She looked a little shocked when I asked her; yet when I told her that I would be praying for her, her eyes softened. She left with my home number, the name of my church, and a promise that I would be praying for her.

Week 2   John 2

The First Sign Is Revealed

People Introduced
Mary (Mother of Christ): Read more about Mary and the virgin birth in the other Gospels (Matthew 1:18–24; Luke 1:26–56).

> *His mother said to the servants, "Whatever He says to you, do it."*
> —John 2:5

John 2:1–12

In John 2, we find Jesus at a wedding along with His mother and disciples. I can imagine Him simply enjoying the festivities with some friends, when His thoughts were interrupted by a request from none other than His mom. The wine had run out at the party, and His mother, Mary, apparently felt that this problem needed to be addressed and that she knew Someone who could do something about it. However, when she mentioned the situation to Jesus (both her son and Son of God), she received a peculiar response.

 How did Christ respond to His mother's statement (v. 4)?

Woman! To our modern ears, the way the word *woman* is used in this sentence sounds a little disrespectful. If I heard a young man answer his mother today by saying, "Woman, I told you...," I would likely be appalled at what I would have perceived as his display of disrespect. However, many biblical scholars suggest that the word *woman* used this way was not derogatory but a traditional way in which a Jewish man in that period would have addressed an adult woman. So let us move on to the end of His comment, which contains something worth pondering. Christ told His mother that her concern was not an issue He needed to deal with, and that it was not time yet to reveal His identity as God. Specifically, He stated, *"My hour has not yet come"* (John 2:4).

 Read the following verses, and discuss the common thread.

So they were seeking to seize Him; and no man laid his hand on Him, because His hour had not yet come.
—John 7:30

These words He spoke in the treasury, as He taught in the temple; and no one seized Him, because His hour had not yet come.
—John 8:20

And Jesus answered them, saying, "The hour has come for the Son of Man to be glorified."
—John 12:23

"Now My soul has become troubled; and what shall I say, 'Father, save Me from this hour'? But for this purpose I came to this hour."
—John 12:27

Now before the Feast of the Passover, Jesus knowing that His hour had come that He would depart out of this world to the Father, having loved His own who were in the world, He loved them to the end.
—John 13:1

Jesus spoke these things; and lifting up His eyes to heaven, He said, "Father, the hour has come; glorify Your Son, that the Son may glorify You."
—John 17:1

Throughout the Gospel of John, we see that Jesus often gave reference to the *hour* or *time*, which was evidently approaching. Christ was referring to the time of His sacrificial death on the Cross and His subsequent resurrection from the dead. From the beginning of His earthly ministry, Christ had the Cross on His mind; we see this through His escape from pursuers early on in His ministry (John 7:30; 8:20) to His later prediction of His own death (John 12:32–33). These verses illustrate the fact that God has all things in control. Though Christ lived life day by day as a human while on earth, He, in His deity, was well aware of the divine reason His feet ever touched earthen soil. We, as believers, can find immeasurable rest and cause to rejoice in this fact. The God we serve not only existed before all time but also enacted a plan for our redemption before the foundation of time—a plan that brought God to earth in the form of the Son, allowed Him to dwell among man, and caused Him to remain faithful to our need to the point of self-sacrifice on the Cross. He alone was able to attempt such a feat, for only God could come into a sinful world and remain spotless. And only God could have perfect future vision to ensure that His plan would succeed. For not only could He see the future, but His very hands governed every act.

Although Christ's hour had not yet come, there in Cana of Galilee, His first miracle was performed. In John's account of the water being changed into wine, we are not told that everyone at the wedding realized that a miracle had taken place there. After all, this was not the primary purpose. However, some people did benefit from witnessing this miracle.

 According to the following verse, what were two results of Jesus's miracle of changing the water into wine?

This beginning of His signs Jesus did in Cana of Galilee, and manifested His glory, and His disciples believed in Him.
—John 2:11

Christ's miracle at the wedding served to bring Him glory and strengthen the faith of His disciples. Note that although not everyone at the wedding was aware of the miracle that had taken place, Christ still displayed His glory. Christ's glory is not dependent upon our recognition of Him as Lord and Savior; yet our salvation is crucially dependent upon that very fact.

John 2:13–25

Often in society, Jesus is portrayed as a meek, mild-tempered man who walked humbly upon the earth to teach us love, while never speaking a harsh word. Well, I have no clue from where this concept was derived. Yes, Jesus was meek and, yes, He was humble, but the Scriptures give us clear accounts of a Man who was not afraid to speak out against things He deemed unholy. His encounter with the money changers and marketers at the Temple provides a vivid example that Jesus Christ did not meander around sin.

> *And He made a scourge of cords, and drove them all out of the temple, with the sheep and the oxen; and He poured out the coins of the money changers and overturned their tables; and to those who were selling the doves He said, "Take these things away; stop making My Father's house a place of business."*
> —John 2:15–16

 Discuss the situation Christ encountered upon His arrival at the Temple (vv. 13–16).

Yearly, persons of the Jewish faith would travel to Jerusalem to celebrate Passover. This was a time of remembrance of God's faithfulness in the past, worship, anticipation for the coming Messiah, and sacrifice for sins. People were expected to bring an animal to be offered as a sacrifice for their sin. Seeing an opportunity for profit, marketers and money changers moved their stations into the temple grounds in order to benefit from this sacred ceremony.

Christ did not casually stroll into the area and quietly suggest that they stop these practices. Instead, He made a whip of cords and took action. This had to have been a sight to behold—tables being overturned, animals fleeing, upset entrepreneurs gathering their goods! Yet in the midst of the excitement, Christ made a statement that once more identified Him: *"Stop making My Father's house a place of business"* (John 2:16).

Without reservation, Christ boldly proclaimed the Temple of God as His Father's house. This probably perked up some ears. The Jews were expecting a coming Messiah, but not necessarily a raving man sweeping through the Temple with a cord of whips to run off those making the Temple a place of merchandising. So, naturally, they asked Him to prove His claim.

> *The Jews then said to Him, "What sign do You show us as your authority for doing these things?" Jesus answered them, "Destroy this temple, and in three days I will raise it up." The Jews then said, "It took forty-six years to build this temple, and will You raise it up in three days?" But He was speaking of the temple of His body.*
> —John 2:18–21

 What sign or promise did Jesus Christ offer the accusers (v. 19)?

Jesus's statement had to be confusing. His listeners were standing in the middle of a courtyard attached to the Temple that had taken 46 years so far to build. Then this Man named Jesus claimed that if *"this temple"* were destroyed, He would *"raise it up"* in only three days. Unfortunately, like most of us, His listeners were so caught up in the physical world around them, that they could not understand the truth behind Christ's words.

 What "temple" was Christ referring to in His response (v. 21)?

Christ was alluding to future events: His death and resurrection. At Christ's death, the sin debt was paid. Thus, yearly sacrifices would no longer be required on behalf of people. A building made with hands would no longer be necessary to represent the presence of God. Instead, Christ's sacrifice was a once-and-for-all, sufficient payment for sin. He came to be the Temple, the place of sacrifice, the ultimate sacrifice. This concept was confusing even to His disciples, who walked daily with Him. John 2:22 states that it was not until after Christ was raised from the dead that His disciples who had heard this statement *"believed the Scripture and the word which Jesus had spoken."* What they, at first, could not fully understand became quite clear at

Christ's resurrection from the dead. They were not privy to the 20/20 hindsight we all now enjoy. As believers today, we are given better hindsight through the study of the Scriptures and guidance of the Holy Spirit. We have the whole story; we must simply believe.

Personal Reflection

1. **What signs am I asking God for so that I can fully place my faith in Christ?**

2. **In what ways has my life caused Christ to be angry about my actions? What are some "money changer tables" that need to be overturned in my life today?**

The Word in the World

Sharon: Question to the Point of Receiving

One Sunday, I asked members of my Sunday School class to fill out a simple form that encouraged them to be honest about their relationship with Jesus Christ or lack of the same. To my surprise, Sharon marked that she was not sure whether she was a Christian. Sharon had grown up on the foreign mission field, and she came from a strong Christian family.

The following weekend, Sharon and some other girls went to a girls' conference with me. We all stayed together in a huge hotel room. When I saw an opportunity, I seized it and asked Sharon to step outside with me to talk. She shared how she often felt that the Christian culture was her parents' thing, but she did not know if she really believed it for herself. As we read through the Scriptures, she came to the point that she wanted to "make it real" for her own life. I had the honor of praying with her as she received Christ as her Lord—as she was born into the family of God!

Week 3   John 3

God So Loved the World

People Introduced

Nicodemus (a Pharisee, a Jewish religious leader similar to a modern priest or rabbi)

Jesus answered and said to him, "Truly, truly, I say to you, unless one is born again he cannot see the kingdom of God."
—John 3:3

John 3:1–21

In John 3, we are introduced to Nicodemus, a ruler of the Jews and a Pharisee. According to biblical history, a Pharisee was one who devoted much of his life to the study of the Torah (the first five books of the Old Testament and the basis for Jewish law). Therefore, Nicodemus was not naïve about religion. Possibly it was his inquisitive mind that drove him to seek to discover more about this Man called Jesus.

 Read John 3:2–3. When did Nicodemus visit Jesus?

Nicodemus approached Jesus at night. Although the Scriptures do not give us a clear reason as to why he chose this timing, I believe that it is within the realm of reason to assume that Nicodemus did not want his meeting with Jesus to be made public. He belonged to a group that did not embrace the teachings of Christ; yet he had a personal interest in understanding more about Him. This interest drove him to meet with Jesus alone. Upon their meeting, Nicodemus not only addressed Jesus as "Rabbi" (the Jewish term for teacher) but also went further by stating his belief that Jesus was sent by God. The basis of this belief was the miraculous signs that had been witnessed up to this point. Once Christ received these confessions from Nicodemus, He made a statement that proved to be confusing to His visitor.

How did Jesus reply to Nicodemus's confessions?

Jesus told Nicodemus, *"Unless one is born again he cannot see the kingdom of God"* (John 3:3). Nicodemus, like many today, found Jesus's statement a little perplexing. Because of his understanding of the physical birth, he compared being born again with the impossible act of someone reentering his or her mother's womb to be born a second time. Christ then repeated His previous statement and went on to explain a difference between those born of flesh and those born of the Spirit. The second birth would be a spiritual occurrence.

Just as individuals having undergone physical birth demonstrate traits resembling their origins, so do those who have experienced spiritual birth. Children typically share features found in their parents, such as hair and eye color. Children born of God through the second birth also share in a spiritual nature that can be derived only from Him. Unlike physical characteristics, which can be seen with the eye, touched with the hand, or easily recognized through the senses, spiritual characteristics are commonly recognized through the results they bring.

Discuss the analogy Jesus made regarding the wind and those born of Spirit (v. 8).

"The wind blows where it wishes and you hear the sound of it, but do not know where it comes from and where it is going; so is everyone who is born of the Spirit."
—John 3:8

At this point in John 3, we are about to really get into the gospel, or good news. Jesus compared Himself with the serpent that Moses lifted up in the wilderness as a promise of God and so that the lives of all who gazed upon that serpent would be saved (Numbers 21:9). Nicodemus, having studied the books of Law, which are in the Old Testament, would have known this story well. However, he would not necessarily have understood Jesus's next comparison. Jesus Christ attributed to Himself the title *Son of Man*, stating, *"Even so must the Son of Man be lifted up; so that whoever believes will in Him have eternal life"* (John 3:14–15). With this, Christ was boldly declaring that He is the source of hope for eternal life.

 Read aloud John 3:16–17. What is the promise given to those who look only to the Son of God, Jesus Christ, for their hope of salvation?

"For God so loved the world, that He gave His only begotten Son, that whoever believes in Him shall not perish, but have eternal life. For God did not send the Son into the world to judge the world, but that the world might be saved through Him."
—John 3:16–17

Out of God's love for the world, He sent *"His only begotten Son,"* Jesus Christ, so that anyone who places his or her faith in Him will be saved. Those who trust in Jesus Christ as their Savior are released from their prior destiny of eternal separation from God and, instead, given the privilege of becoming children of God, the privilege of dwelling in His presence. Christ's life, death, and resurrection from the dead took place not to condemn the world but rather, to provide an escape from God's wrath through faith in Him.

 How does your personal faith in Jesus Christ affect your standing before God in regard to condemnation (v. 18; provided in two translations)?

"Whoever believes in him is not condemned, but whoever does not believe stands condemned already because he has not believed in the name of God's one and only Son."
—John 3:18 (NIV)

"He who believes in Him is not judged; he who does not believe has been judged already, because he has not believed in the name of the only begotten Son of God."
—John 3:18 (NASB)

Those of us who have placed our faith in Jesus Christ as our Savior no longer have to fear the condemnation of God. However, those who have not done so stand condemned already. It is commonly thought that to offend God, someone must do something really bad, such as curse His name out loud in blatant defiance or kill someone. However, verse 18 makes a clear and weighty proclamation: all a person must do to be condemned is simply not believe in God's Son, Jesus Christ. This truth ought to bring chills even to those who know Christ as Savior. Eternal separation from God is not merely a result of living a life deemed horrible by society; rather, eternal separation is possible through a quiet unwillingness to bend from pride and look to God's Son for salvation.

 According to what you have just studied, what would be the outcome of living a good life without a personal faith and relationship with Jesus Christ?

Christ stated that *"the Light"* had come into the world, but the people loved the darkness instead (v. 19). Darkness can be comfortable. Sins and faults can remain hidden in the dark, yet light causes them to be revealed. In the same way that some insects comfortably abide in a darkened room but run when exposed to sudden light, many of us want to run from that which exposes us, hoping to find a place to hide ourselves—away from the source of exposure. The light of Christ causes exposure. When faced with the Word of God, we are enlightened to our sin and our need for salvation. It is then that we must decide whether to run from the light or to stand in the light, acknowledge what the light shows us, and receive cleansing and healing.

John 3:22–30

As we read John 3:22–30, we get another glimpse into the life of John the Baptist. According to these verses, John was continuing his work as the forerunner for

Christ during the same time that Jesus began baptizing people in Judea. These dual baptisms caused some confusion among people and led to John being approached about the issue. John was told that many people were flocking to Jesus for baptism.

 How does John's response, as recorded in the following passage, represent his understanding and acknowledgment that he himself was not the Christ (the Messiah)?

John answered and said, "A man can receive nothing unless it has been given him from heaven. You yourselves are my witnesses that I said, 'I am not the Christ,' but, 'I have been sent ahead of Him.' He who has the bride is the bridegroom; but the friend of the bridegroom, who stands and hears him, rejoices greatly because of the bridegroom's voice. So this joy of mine has been made full. He must increase, but I must decrease."
—John 3:27–30

When approached by those concerned about so many people going to Jesus for baptism, John was not distressed. He quickly replied once again that he himself was not the Messiah but had been sent ahead of the Messiah (v. 28); this had been his testimony all along. Instead of becoming jealous or angry about the beginning of Jesus's public ministry, John said that his joy had been made full (v. 29). John had the privilege of seeing his ministry coming to its end. The One about whom he had been testifying was now becoming public. John ended his answer with the statement, *"He must increase, but I must decrease"* (John 3:30). He recognized that the focus must be off him and fully on Christ.

John 3:31–36

The final six verses of John 3 provide more insight into Jesus Christ. He is referred to as *"He who comes from above"* (v. 31). This tells us that Christ is from heaven; thus, He possesses all the attributes associated with that standing.

Read aloud the following passage. List attributes given to Christ in these verses.

"He who comes from above is above all, he who is of the earth is from the earth and speaks of the earth. He who comes from heaven is above all. What He has seen and heard, of that He testifies; and no one receives His testimony. He who has received His testimony has set his seal to this, that God is true. For He whom God has sent speaks the words of God; for He gives the Spirit without measure. The Father loves the Son and has given all things into His hand."
—John 3:31–35

We are told that God has placed all things into the hands of Christ, His Son. God is well pleased with His Son and has lavishly bestowed wisdom, power, and authority upon Him. An aspect of Christ's complete authority (Matthew 28:18) is the fact that all judgment of people is placed in His hands (John 5:22; Acts 17:31). Once again, we read in the Scriptures that faith in Christ is the crux between eternal rest with God and eternal punishment within His wrath.

 How do verses 18 and 36 of John 3 speak to the necessity of faith in Christ?

"Whoever believes in him is not condemned, but whoever does not believe stands condemned already because he has not believed in the name of God's one and only Son."
—John 3:18 (NIV)

"He who believes in the Son has eternal life; but he who does not obey the Son will not see life, but the wrath of God abides on him."
—John 3:36

Personal Reflection

1. **According to John 3, am I currently standing in the freedom of eternal life or in condemnation before God based on my personal belief in or about Jesus Christ?**

2. **How does the knowledge that God has placed all authority of salvation into the hands of Jesus Christ encourage and/or convict my understanding of the importance of faith in Christ?**

The Word in the World

Ashley: I Don't Know Anything About Jesus

While inviting some co-workers to a Bible study at church, I got into a conversation with a young lady named Ashley. She tentatively accepted the invitation with an interesting follow-up statement: "Sure, I may come. But I don't know anything about Jesus." She later said, "I do, however, like to collect Bibles!"

We soon met for lunch and began walking together through the Book of John. One month later, during our study of the fourth chapter of John, Ashley placed her faith in Christ as her Savior! We continued through the rest of the book, and it was exciting to watch her grow!

Jesus Offers Living Water

Jesus answered and said to her, "Everyone who drinks of this water will thirst again; but whoever drinks of the water that I will give him shall never thirst; but the water that I will give him will become in him a well of water springing up to eternal life."
—John 4:13–14

John 4:1–42

Envision with me that hot, dusty day. Jesus and His disciples had been traveling from Judea toward Galilee. Jesus, demonstrating the realities of His earthly body, became tired and wanted to rest His aching feet. This moment of rest turned into a divine opportunity for Christ to demonstrate His willingness to break with culture.

At this point in their journey, Jesus and His disciples had come to a Samaritan town by the name of Sychar. It is important to note that, historically, most Jews of proper breeding did not associate with Samaritans, looking on them as a lower class of people because they had mixed Jewish/Gentile ancestry. However, while His disciples went further into the city in search of food, Christ decided to rest at a local well, which had been dug over a thousand years before by Jacob (a great Jewish leader written about in the Old Testament.)

There Christ encountered a Samaritan woman who had come to the well to draw water. According to verse 6, the time was around the sixth hour, which might place the event around noonday, right in the heat of the day. This timing is particularly interesting because most women chose the early morning or late evening hours to come to the well in order to avoid the heat of the day. This woman, possibly driven by shame and her desire to avoid public contact, chose to come at midday. Her decision to avoid the scrutiny of many led her straight into the path of the only One who could rightly be her Judge.

Immediately breaking with tradition, Jesus asked the woman for a drink of water. Obviously shocked, the woman began questioning why He spoke to her. Being the Master of analogies, Christ replied, *"If you knew the gift of God, and who it is who says to you, 'Give Me a drink,' you would have asked Him, and He would have given you living water"* (John 4:10). Not understanding His response, the woman began to point out the obvious.

> *She said to Him, "Sir, You have nothing to draw with and the well is deep; where then do You get that living water?"*
> —John 4:11

 How does verse 11 demonstrate that the Samaritan woman did not understand the full meaning of Christ's statement?

Like many of us today, the Samaritan woman had trouble seeing beyond the obvious—things that can be touched and observed with the eyes. She reminded Christ that He did not have a bucket, cup, or anything with which to draw water from the well. She then began to compare Him with Jacob, a founder of the Jewish faith—and evidently her faith—not recognizing that the ultimate fulfillment of her faith sat before her. It is so easy for us to focus on what we have learned through tradition and practice, while completely missing out on a relationship with Christ. The future Messiah, to whom Jacob had looked forward, was at that very moment sitting before her, and all she could see was the practical.

 Discuss the potential dangers of *knowing about Christ* rather than actually *knowing Christ as your Savior.*

Referring to the physical water before Him, Christ explained that those who drank from that well would temporarily have their thirst quenched. However, He alone offers *"living water"* (Himself), which, when accepted, forever quenches the thirstiness of one's soul (vv. 10, 14).

We are all composed of a physical body and a spiritual essence. Just as our bodies crave food and water, our souls, or inner selves, have cravings. Imagine a line drawn vertically down the middle of your body. One half represents your physical self; the other is your soul, or inner self. Food and water are essential to meet the needs of your physical half. Christ alone is essential to meet the deepest needs of the other. Until you have a personal relationship with Christ, you will experience a hunger or thirst that cannot be permanently satisfied.

 List ways you have sought to temporarily quench your spiritual thirst and satisfy your spiritual hunger.

Christ, leading up to a demonstration of who He is, told the woman to do something impossible: to go call her husband. The woman confessed she did not have a husband (v. 17). To that statement, Christ replied that she was right, that she had had five husbands and the man she was living with at the time was not her husband (vv. 17–18). Realizing that He could not have known this through natural means, she immediately replied, *"Sir, I perceive that You are a prophet"* (John 4:19). The woman had moved a step closer to the truth, but still needed further clarification of who Jesus truly is.

 Read aloud John 4:21–26. Explain the purpose of worshipping God in spirit and truth.

Jesus said to her, "Woman, believe Me, an hour is coming when neither in this mountain nor in Jerusalem will you worship the Father. You worship what you do not know; we worship what we know, for salvation is from the Jews. But an hour is coming, and now is, when the true worshipers will worship the Father in spirit and truth; for such people the Father seeks to be His worshipers. God is spirit, and those who worship Him must worship in spirit and truth." The

woman said to Him, "I know that Messiah is coming (He who is called Christ); when that One comes, He will declare all things to us." Jesus said to her, "I who speak to you am He."
—John 4:21–26

The cultural norms came crashing down. Jesus was speaking not only to a Samaritan but a woman at that! He found her worthy not only of conversation but also of truth and salvation. Christ explained to her that a time was coming in which *"true worshipers"* would worship God not simply through history and tradition but through truth (the Scriptures) and spirit (the indwelling presence of the Holy Spirit in the lives of believers). Recognizing some familiar ring of truth in His statement, the woman replied, *"I know that Messiah is coming (He who is called Christ); when that One comes, He will declare all things to us"* (John 4:25). To this, Christ replied, *"I who speak to you am He"* (v. 26). Leaving no room for misunderstanding, Christ declared Himself to be the Messiah for whom those of the Jewish faith had been waiting.

Can you imagine how this woman must have felt? Most likely, due to her history of having multiple husbands and lovers, she was not the most popular woman in town. Her reputation was less than pristine and had driven her to doing daily duties, such as drawing water from the well, during times of the day that would not allow for much public interaction. Then there she was—she, of all people—speaking to the Messiah, the Savior of the world! This is a wonderful illustration of how God is not put off by our past failures; rather He is interested in our futures, which are determined by our willingness to come to Him in faith. We bring nothing to His feet; yet there, we find everything we need.

 Consider any events in your own life that have caused you to feel too inferior to approach Christ. How can the illustration of the Samaritan woman encourage you to draw near to Christ?

Upon her recognition of Christ, the woman quickly left the well and went to tell the people in her town. Her exit was so sudden that she even left her water jar. The news she had to share was exciting! The Savior of the world, the Messiah, had come.

She knew little else than that she had spoken with Christ, the Messiah, and this was enough to cause her to abandon all and run with the good news.

 Read the following verses aloud. What was the result of this woman's testimony?

From that city many of the Samaritans believed in Him because of the word of the woman who testified, "He told me all the things that I have done." So when the Samaritans came to Jesus, they were asking Him to stay with them; and He stayed there two days. Many more believed because of His word; and they were saying to the woman, "It is no longer because of what you said that we believe, for we have heard for ourselves and know that this One is indeed the Savior of the world."
—John 4:39–42

We are not told that the Samaritan woman had a grand testimony. We are told only that she had an encounter with Christ. An encounter that left her with a vigorous faith that she dared to share with those in her hometown. Although her testimony drew those in the town toward an interest in Christ, for many, their faith was not complete until after they met Him themselves. What began as a countercultural event ended as an opportunity to use one ordinary woman's testimony to draw many toward a relationship with Jesus Christ.

John 4:43–54

In these next verses, we find Jesus reaching His intended destination of Galilee. We are told that the Galileans welcomed Him freely because they had seen everything He had done in Jerusalem. Upon returning to the city of Cana (where He had turned the water into wine), Christ was approached by a royal official who was in desperate need.

 What event drove this official to seek Christ (v. 47)?

Notice that when the man heard that Jesus had entered Galilee, he went to Him. This official was so eager that he sought out Christ. Upon finding Him, he pleaded with Christ to go to his son and heal him. You can hear the urgency in his voice through the words, *"Sir, come down before my child dies"* (John 4:49). Obviously, the official had previously decided that Jesus must be physically present, touch the boy, or somehow be near in order to heal him. Therefore, Christ's response to him demanded much more faith:

> *Jesus said to him, "Go; your son lives." The man believed the word that Jesus spoke to him and started off.*
> —John 4:50

 Why did Jesus's command, *"Go,"* require more faith than if Jesus had followed the official to his son's bedside (v. 50)?

After being told to go and that his son would live, the man departed. He had to trust Jesus's words. It is much easier to believe when we can physically see something with our eyes. I am sure that the father would have had more immediate peace about the matter if he could have dragged Jesus with him to the boy's bed. However, Christ demanded that he have faith in His words. I can imagine that he possibly left a little disappointed. This was evidently not how the official had planned the encounter to end. Yet, despite his feelings, he obeyed Christ and headed home.

> *As he was now going down, his slaves met him, saying that his son was living. So he inquired of them the hour when he began to get better. Then they said to him, "Yesterday at the seventh hour the fever left him." So the father knew that it was at that hour in which Jesus said to him, "Your son lives," and he himself believed and his whole household.*
> —John 4:51–53

 What is the significance of the conversation between the official and his slaves concerning the timing of his son's healing (vv. 51–53)?

While being forced to literally walk in faith, the official was met by his slaves who pronounced that his son was alive. When he inquired about the time his son was healed, he was told that it was the exact time of his meeting with Christ. Confirmation that Jesus was trustworthy was provided to one who exercised faith in Him. Because of this, the man and his household placed their complete faith in Christ.

Personal Reflection

1. **Is my faith in Christ dependent upon what someone else has told me about Him? Or can I truly say what the Samaritans said: I *"have heard for [myself] and know that this One is indeed the Savior of the world"* (John 4:42)?**

2. **What are the boundaries in my life that restrict me from sharing my faith as openly as did the woman at the well?**

The Word in the World

One Sows and Another Reaps

Sometimes when we share, we see God move immediately. Other times, we are left to simply trust that His Word never returns void. By sharing, we may be planting seeds or reaping the benefits of someone else's planting. We never know until we share. Both positions are invaluable. So, in this knowledge, share on!

> Jesus said to them, "*My food is to do the will of Him who sent Me and to accomplish His work. Do you not say, 'There are yet four months, and then comes the harvest'? Behold, I say to you, lift up your eyes and look on the fields, that they are white for harvest. Already he who reaps is receiving wages and is gathering fruit for life eternal; so that he who sows and he who reaps may rejoice together. For in this case the saying is true, 'One sows and another reaps.' I sent you to reap that for which you have not labored; others have labored and you have entered into their labor.*"
> —John 4:34–38

Week 5 　 John 5

Jesus Heals

People Introduced
Sick man of Bethesda

When Jesus saw him lying there, and knew that he had already been a long time in that condition, He said to him, "Do you wish to get well?" The sick man answered Him, "Sir, I have no man to put me into the pool when the water is stirred up, but while I am coming, another steps down before me." Jesus said to him, "Get up, pick up your pallet and walk."
—John 5:6–8

John 5:1–15
Some time later after Jesus's trip through Samaria to Galilee, Jesus returned to Jerusalem for a feast of the Jews.

Now there is in Jerusalem by the sheep gate a pool, which is called in Hebrew Bethesda, having five porticoes. In these lay a multitude of those who were sick, blind, lame, and withered, [waiting for the moving of the waters; for an angel of the Lord went down at certain seasons into the pool and stirred up the water; whoever then first, after the stirring up of the water, stepped in was made well from whatever disease with which he was afflicted.] A man was there who had been ill for thirty-eight years.
—John 5:2–5

Describe the scene Jesus encountered at the sheep gate in Jerusalem (John 5:2–5)?

The pool of Bethesda was anything but a spa resort. Rather than finding well-built men and women lounging around in towels, Christ encountered a mass of broken and hurting people. Desperate to find healing, the blind, lame, and disabled would lie on mats near the pool, anxiously awaiting an angelic stirring of the water. The understanding was that the first person who made it into the pool after the stirring would receive healing. The sights, sounds, and smells of the place must have been overwhelming. The area was a sea of mangled people, all struggling from some sort of ailment, hoping for some miraculous healing. Those who held fervently to this hope would stay for years, desperately desiring some chance of recovery.

 How long had the man Jesus spoke to been ill?

I cannot get over the concept of this man still hoping, having been ill 38 years—lying there day after day, desiring to be healed, knowing he had no help to get into the pool should the waters stir. Talk about commitment! We often give up on a prayer request or a hope if it is not fulfilled in 38 days, much less 38 years. This man's desire was obvious: he wanted to be healed. However, when Christ approached him, the first thing He asked him was this: *Do you wish to get well?*" (John 5:6).

 How did the man respond to Jesus's question (v. 7)?

Through this man's response, we see where the foundation of his faith was—it lay within himself or the abilities of others. He clearly understood that alone he could never make it to the water and complained that he had no friends who could carry him there. These are both realistic problems, yet he did not realize that before him was standing the only One who could truly bring him the healing he so desired. The only thing Christ demanded was faith.

Jesus said to him, "Get up, pick up your pallet and walk."
—John 5:8

 Explain the role faith had in the sick man's obedience to the command Christ gave him (v. 8).

The man could have responded in a number of ways. Remember, he had been ill for 38 years. Do you not think that if walking were an option, he would have already tried it? He could have sneered at Jesus's remark and become embittered, thinking, "Sure, go ahead and mock me like the others." Or he could have demanded that others assist him, believing in only his natural, physical limitations. Yet he did none of these. Instead, he *"immediately"* picked up his bedroll and started to walk (v. 9)! His healing occurred not through some mystical stirring of water or great effort on behalf of his friends but rather through his complete faith in the One who said, *"Walk."*

This healing, having occurred on the Sabbath, caused a scandal among the Jewish religious leaders. The Sabbath was considered their Holy Day and law forbade any work—including healing—from being done on that day of the week. When the leaders later discovered that Jesus was the One who had performed this miracle of healing, they were furious and began to seek his persecution (vv. 15–16). Once more, Jesus Christ was seen breaking with tradition and culture. He did not seek to mock or destroy all tradition; rather, He proved that He was not bound by its rules.

John 5:16–47

The next several verses remind us of truths about Christ we have previously learned and introduce us to further knowledge of His character. Although Jesus repeatedly said that He could do nothing apart from the Father (God), He spoke in ways that reinforced His equality with God. Jesus Christ spoke of God as His Father. He never minced words. When Christ spoke of God, His most common term was *Father*, reflecting the extremely personal and equal relationship. Such statements proved to be added fuel for the anger already felt by some of His fellow Jews toward Him.

> *But He answered them, "My Father is working until now, and I Myself am working." For this reason therefore the Jews were seeking all the more to kill Him, because He not only was breaking the Sabbath, but also was calling God His own Father, making Himself equal with*

God. Therefore Jesus answered and was saying to them, "Truly, truly, I say to you, the Son can do nothing of Himself, unless it is something He sees the Father doing; for whatever the Father does, these things the Son also does in like manner. For the Father loves the Son, and shows Him all things that He Himself is doing; and the Father will show Him greater works than these, so that you will marvel. For just as the Father raises the dead and gives them life, even so the Son also gives life to whom He wishes. For not even the Father judges anyone, but He has given all judgment to the Son, so that all will honor the Son even as they honor the Father. He who does not honor the Son does not honor the Father who sent Him.
—John 5:17–23

 How did Christ's response to the accusation of the Jewish officials indicate that He was intentionally calling Himself equal with God (vv. 19–23)?

Picture the scene: Jesus had healed the ill man on the Sabbath, breaking the Sabbath law, and so the Jewish officials began to persecute Him. Well aware of their tradition and laws, He proceeded to refer to Himself as the Son of God in His response to the officials. If Jesus had been looking for a way to excuse or hide His identity, this term would not have been the best choice. The Scriptures do not indicate that Jesus was simply a good man. In opposition to a widely held view of Christ, the Scriptures refute the concept that Jesus lived as a mere example of goodness. He never claimed to be simply a good person. Instead, He claimed to be the Son of God. This is the claim that kept Him before those religious officials, drove people mad who assumed He was mocking God, and eventually secured Him a place on a wooden cross.

 Compare the role of Christ as found in John 3:16 with that identified in John 5:24.

"For God so loved the world, that He gave His only begotten Son, that whoever believes in Him shall not perish, but have eternal life."
—John 3:16

"Truly, truly, I say to you, he who hears My word, and believes Him who sent Me, has eternal life, and does not come into judgment, but has passed out of death into life."
—John 5:24

Through these verses, we see that belief in Christ as God's Son is the core of our salvation. We are never told that believing that Christ existed is sufficient for salvation. We can believe that someone exists without having a personal relationship with that person. I am convinced that George W. Bush is alive today. I have seen pictures, heard him speak, and feel confident in knowing that he exists. However, if he entered a room where I was and I ran up to him proclaiming, "I knew you were real," security guards would most assuredly quickly accost me. The reason being, although I know who he is cognitively, I do not have a personal relationship with the man. As individuals, we must each make a personal decision of faith concerning the claims of Jesus Christ. In order for salvation to occur, our individual understanding of Him must move from seeing Him as a man who once existed to acknowledging Him to be the perfect Son of God who lived, died, and arose from the grave as the ultimate sacrifice for sin.

In John 5:25–29, Jesus began to speak of a future event: There will come a time when He will return and call each of us to Himself. Those of us who have placed our faith in Him will go on to spend eternity with Him and God the Father. However, those who have denied Him as Savior will suffer eternity apart from the presence of God. In the latter part of this passage, He was speaking specifically about those who are in the grave, including all who have ever existed. All mankind will eventually be judged by Christ and demanded an account of their actions and foundation of faith. According to the verses we have previously read, faith other than in Christ alone is not sufficient for eternal salvation.

 How does the information in John 5:35–36 about John the Baptist compare with what you have previously learned about him?

"[John] was the lamp that was burning and was shining and you were willing to rejoice for a while in his light. But the testimony which I have is greater than the testimony of John; for the works which the Father has given Me to accomplish—the very works that I do—testify about Me, that the Father has sent Me.
—John 5:35–36

The Scriptures repeatedly build upon themselves. This is one reason it is crucial that we study the Scriptures fully. Just as when you hear someone speaking on the phone and you are privy to only one side of the story, randomly picking your way through the Scriptures may allow for critical issues and correlations to be missed or, worse, misinterpreted.

Jesus confirmed John the Baptist's testimony. However, in John 5:36, Jesus went on to say that He had a testimony greater than John's, because the works He was doing testified about Him, that the Father (God) sent Him. Just as John was sent to prepare people to listen to the message of Christ, Christ's works and words were given to prepare us to hear from God.

 According to the following passage, what is the relationship between the Scriptures and Christ?

"And the Father who sent Me, He has testified of Me. You have neither heard His voice at any time nor seen His form. You do not have His word abiding in you, for you do not believe Him whom He sent. You search the Scriptures because you think that in them you have eternal life; it is these that testify about Me; and you are unwilling to come to Me so that you may have life."
—John 5:37–40

Remember that this speech was given before the religious officials. They had devoutly studied the Scriptures and believed that through their study they would obtain salvation and eternal life. Standing before them, Jesus daringly said, *"You search the Scriptures because you think that in them you have eternal life; it is these that testify about Me; and you are unwilling to come to Me so that you may have life"* (John 5:39–40). Any room for confusion seems to evaporate. Christ, once more, clearly states that He is the purpose of the Scriptures and the source of salvation. A serious warning is also found in this statement: It is possible to know much about the Scriptures and not have a relationship with Jesus Christ. Study alone does not produce salvation. Each of us must be willing to come to Christ. Salvation is found through a personal relationship with a personal Savior, not merely through head knowledge.

 Read the passage that follows and describe the danger Christ spoke of regarding placing hope in Moses rather than in his teachings of the coming Messiah.

"Do not think that I will accuse you before the Father; the one who accuses you is Moses, in whom you have set your hope. For if you believed Moses, you would believe Me, for he wrote about Me. But if you do not believe his writings, how will you believe My words?"
—John 5:45–47

Cutting to the marrow of the religious leaders' traditional belief, Christ denounced steadfast hope in a person other than Himself. Moses was used greatly by God in the Old Testament, and his writings proclaim great works and teachings of God. These are essential sources of growth and understanding for the Christian faith, yet they all point toward the arrival and personhood of Jesus Christ. He alone is the center focus, the pivotal point of all the Scriptures. As were those religious leaders, we are in danger when we allow our gazes to focus on great teachers of the Scriptures to the detriment of our relationship with Jesus Christ. Bible teachers, spiritual leaders, heroes of the faith, and mentors can become our accusers when we falsely esteem them higher than Christ.

Personal Reflection

1. **In what areas of my life am I still lying beside the pool of Bethesda waiting for true healing?**

2. **In what ways have I allowed other people to assume the false title of *savior* in my life rather than focusing solely upon Jesus Christ as my Savior?**

The Word in the World

Ella: She Needed the Bread of Life

A patient's chart stated the diagnosis of eating disorder. Sensing God wanting me to talk with the patient, I began to pray that He would open a door.

Moments later, I heard someone call from behind me. I turned around to be met by the patient's mom asking for water. This was it; this was my open door. Then I got scared. Go figure.

"Lord, what am I supposed to say? How do I initiate this conversation?" Finally, I sent up a quick prayer for help and went for it. I introduced myself and told her that I had noticed her daughter's diagnosis. I shared that I had once struggled with a similar issue and would love to speak with her daughter. Surprisingly, she said yes.

Entering the patient's room, I saw a frail young woman lying in the bed. As I moved closer, I began telling her that I, too, had battled with an eating disorder. Hearing this, the look in her eyes changed from suspicion to curiosity.

We had spoken for several minutes when I asked her if she had ever accepted Jesus Christ as her Savior. She said no. I explained that He alone saved my life, and that without Him, I would still be in bondage. This sparked a longer conversation. She expressed a desire to believe but said that for some reason she could not. I shared that Christ promised that if we seek Him, we would find Him. I gave a simple explanation of the gospel and encouraged her, telling her that she had all the tools she needed to make that decision. She said that she would think about it more. I gave her my home phone number and prayed with her. I left that day thanking God that He can use our past "chains" to help free others.

Week 6 · John 6

I Am the Bread of Life

People Introduced

Judas Iscariot (one of the chosen twelve disciples, the one who betrayed Christ)

"I am the living bread that came down out of heaven; if anyone eats of this bread, he will live forever; and the bread also which I will give for the life of the world is My flesh."
—John 6:51

John 6:1–21

By this time, Jesus had attracted a following. Many had heard of or witnessed His miracles firsthand and were beginning to follow Him around, eager to see more. If Jesus had been seeking an opportunity to become famous for signs and wonders, this was His shot. People were noticing Him, following Him, and beginning to crave His attention. This would be a tempting time for anyone to begin to promote a personal agenda. Jesus, however, perfectly pursued His Father's purpose without deviating from the original plan—the plan for Jesus to become the ultimate sacrifice for all sin.

Jesus gave us excellent examples of teaching through any life situation. Upon facing the physical need of the ever-growing crowd that was following Him, Jesus Christ used the opportunity to teach His disciples a lesson about God's faithfulness and provision. Rather than quickly solving the problem Himself, Jesus involved His disciples in order to teach them something they would be urged to remember (Matthew 16:5–9). The lesson began with a simple question.

Therefore Jesus, lifting up His eyes and seeing that a large crowd was coming to Him, said to Philip, "Where are we to buy bread, so that

these may eat?" This He was saying to test him, for He Himself knew
what He was intending to do.
—John 6:5–6

Why did Jesus ask Philip where they would buy bread for the crowd of people?

We are told in verse 6 that Jesus not only already knew the answer to His question but had a plan as well. Through asking Philip the question, He could quickly expose Philip's assessment of the situation as well as open his eyes to a need that Christ was able to supernaturally resolve. Unaware of the impending miracle, the disciple immediately resorted to practical answers.

> *Philip answered Him, "Two hundred denarii worth of bread is not*
> *sufficient for them, for everyone to receive a little."*
> —John 6:7

How did Philip's response expose his view on the possibility of feeding such a large crowd?

Jesus's disciples examined the obvious: a huge crowd plus a small boy's lunch equals not enough food for everyone. How like us to look only at the obvious or practical and ignore the possibility that God just might be using what seems to be infeasible to teach us a lesson.

Having the crowd of more than five thousand sit down on the grass, Christ began to distribute the sacrificial lunch (Matthew 14:18–21). One tiny lunch in the hands of Christ not only filled the stomachs of the multitude but also left a surplus far greater than what was originally offered to Him.

Describe how the crowd reacted to this miracle Jesus performed.

> *Therefore when the people saw the sign which He had performed,*
> *they said, "This is truly the Prophet who is to come into the world."*
> *So Jesus, perceiving that they were intending to come and take Him*

by force to make Him king, withdrew again to the mountain by Himself alone.
—John 6:14–15

Having witnessed this miracle, many in the crowd began to herald Jesus as a promised prophet. Although this title sounded great, Jesus knew that with it came another plan. Because He was accomplishing great things among the people in the crowd, they would soon wish to make Him their king. Again, this would normally be considered an honor. Why would Christ not wish to become the king of that area? A position is honorable only if it falls within the plan of God for your life. Christ knew that His main purpose was to be killed on a cross, not to be praised on an earthly throne. Some of the same people who were singing His praises at this time might possibly have been in the crowd that later hurled insults at Him on a rugged cross.

The disciples left the place of that event and headed across the sea in a boat. A few miles offshore, a storm arose. With boat rocking, waves churning around them, and mist slapping the faces of all aboard, they soon noticed an image walking on the water! Possibly wondering if they had consumed too much salt water, they naturally questioned the legitimacy of what they saw.

Then, when they had rowed about three or four miles, they saw Jesus walking on the sea and drawing near to the boat; and they were frightened. But He said to them, "It is I; do not be afraid." So they were willing to receive Him into the boat, and immediately the boat was at the land to which they were going.
—John 6:19–21

 What occurred that encouraged the disciples to allow Christ on board with them?

He spoke to them. A simple statement, *"It is I; do not be afraid,"* identified Christ's presence and calmed all fears. Even when sight was uncertain, His voice was unmistakable. Ears tuned into Christ result from having spent time with Him. Although situations occur in which we cannot always "see" the purpose, we can trust the voice of God, which we learn from knowing His Word.

John 6:22–59

The next day, the crowd pursued Christ to the other side of the sea. Having had their physical hunger satisfied, the people in the crowd longed to continue in their satiation. Yet, true to His form, Christ used this apparent need to point them toward a deeper need:

> *"Do not work for the food which perishes, but for the food which endures to eternal life, which the Son of Man will give to you, for on Him the Father, God, has set His seal."*
> —John 6:27

 Discuss this command of Christ that employs the analogy of eternal food.

Christ exhorted the people following Him to work not merely for food that spoils but for "food" that lasts for eternal life. Seeing their dedication to follow Him across a sea just for some bread and fish, He challenged them to redirect this energy toward something with eternal value. The work that God demands of us is to *"believe in Him whom [God] has sent,"* Jesus Christ (John 6:29). The consumption of a piece of bread allows for a momentary reprieve of physical hunger, but belief in Christ provides eternal satisfaction for all spiritual hunger. Christ alone is the only source of spiritual food that will permanently erase our spiritual hunger and thirst. In order to attain this, we must only believe in Him.

 After reading the following passage, list some promises given to those who profess their faith in Christ.

> *Jesus said to them, "I am the bread of life; he who comes to Me will not hunger, and he who believes in Me will never thirst. But I said to you that you have seen Me, and yet do not believe. All that the Father gives Me will come to Me, and the one who comes to Me I will certainly not cast out. For I have come down from heaven, not to do My own will, but the will of Him who sent Me. This is the will of Him who sent Me, that of all that He has given Me I lose nothing,*

but raise it up on the last day. For this is the will of My Father, that everyone who beholds the Son and believes in Him will have eternal life, and I Myself will raise him up on the last day."
—John 6:35–40

Those of us who profess faith in Christ are granted assurance that we will forever be placed within the eternal grasp of God. The hunger and thirst in our souls will be satisfied, we cannot be cast out of God's presence, and death has ultimately been defeated. Although each of us will eventually face a physical death, those who have placed their faith in Christ are promised that they will be raised up to Him. In other words, we will spend eternity in heaven with Him.

These strong statements began to make the crowd uneasy. After all, they knew where Jesus came from physically, but then He began to claim that He came from heaven. It was all fun and games when He was meeting their physical desires, but once He began to address more serious areas of need, their guards began to rise. He spoke of being the *"bread of life"* (v. 48) and of the importance of "eating" His flesh (v. 51). To this, they argued, "How is this possible?" (v. 52).

> *"I am the living bread that came down out of heaven; if anyone eats of this bread, he will live forever; and the bread also which I will give for the life of the world is My flesh."*
> —John 6:51

 Explain the analogy given in verse 51.

Christ called Himself *"the living bread."* The consumption of Him results in eternal life. At the end of verse 51, Christ called this bread of life His *flesh*. We must "consume" His flesh through the act of accepting Him by faith to be who He claimed to be: the Son of God. Christ came physically, in the flesh, to earth. He was born, grew to adulthood, and lived and breathed on this earth. His flesh was given to the world through His sacrificial act of being crucified on a cross. Note that He said, *"I will give,"* when referring to His flesh. Christ was not nailed to a cross against His will. Rather, He intentionally allowed Himself to be crucified in order that a perfect atonement could be made for the sin of all mankind. His flesh is the eternal bread of life for all who accept Him.

John 6:60–71

I love when the Scriptures record revealing remarks from fellow believers. Upon hearing Christ speak of His body as the bread of life, many of His disciples proclaimed, *"This is a difficult statement; who can listen to it?"* (John 6:60). What a refreshing reminder that Christ was speaking to common, everyday, ordinary people like you and me. Even those who had walked alongside Him were originally confused with this teaching.

In response to their confusion, Christ reminded them that His teachings are not fleshly but spiritual in nature. Therefore, we must rely on God's help in order to understand them. Human wisdom is limited in its attempts to discern the teachings of Christ. It is God who draws us to Him. Any desire we have or effort we make to know God and seek Christ results from the working of Him in us.

Unfortunately, when times get tough and confusing, people want to leave. Once the fanfare, signs, and wonders stopped and people were confronted, instead, with the foundations of truth, some decided it was better to walk away rather than trust. Jesus, therefore, questioned His twelve chosen disciples as to their decision.

 How did Simon Peter's response illustrate His understanding of who Christ is?

Simon Peter answered Him, "Lord, to whom shall we go? You have words of eternal life. We have believed and have come to know that You are the Holy One of God."
—John 6:68–69

Simon Peter responded with a declaration of belief. He declared that Christ has the words of life, and that He is the *"Holy One of God."* However, not all of the Twelve responded this way. Although God had chosen all, one had a unique purpose.

What was the role of Judas Iscariot (v. 71)?

Christ knew that among His closest circle of friends was the very one who would later betray Him to His death. Although He did not reveal Judas's identity at the time, this announcement would serve later to remind the others that Judas's actions had already been predicted. But notice that Jesus said, *"Did I Myself not choose you?"* (John 6:70). Christ chose not only the disciples who would be the first to go out and preach the gospel after His resurrection from the dead but also the one who would betray Him! Not one aspect of His life or death was incidental. The purpose for His arrival to earth—our salvation—was planned from all eternity.

Personal Reflection

1. **Is my faith in Christ at the point where I could honestly echo Simon Peter's question and declaration: *"Lord, to whom shall we go? You have words of eternal life"* (John 6:68)?**

2. **What are the hard truths that God is trying to teach me that I have yet to surrender to or accept?**

The Word in the World

Dr. Jones: How Could An Intelligent Person Believe?

One day, seemingly out of the blue, Dr. Jones began to question my faith in God. In front of a growing crowd of co-workers, he asked how anyone of any intelligence could believe in "some book." I answered him the best I could, stating that faith and reason do not always have to be divorced. We continued for several moments, and as our conversation wound down, he stated his opinion that Christianity is "a modern-day cult." I stated that if he defined a cult as having faith in a holy God who, despite the sin of mankind, sent His only Son as a perfect sacrifice so that we might have not only a relationship with Him here on earth but also an eternity with Him in heaven, then yes, I am a member of this cult called Christianity.

I gave him a copy of *The Case for Faith* by Lee Strobel and told him that I would be praying for him.

Who Is This Jesus?

People Introduced
Jesus's brothers

Then Jesus cried out in the temple, teaching and saying, "You both know Me and know where I am from; and I have not come of Myself, but He who sent Me is true, whom you do not know."
—John 7:28

John 7:1–36

Time was not an elusive element to Christ. In the first verses of this chapter, we are reminded once again that Christ is awaiting His appointed time to be arrested by the national officials. From the initial moment that His feet touched this earth, Christ had a specific time planned to die for our sin. Nothing about His life was accidental. Every conversation, encounter, trial, and even persecution were divinely planned by God in order to ensure the success of His perfect plan to rescue mankind from the bondage of sin.

Although Jesus Christ's timing was perfect, the understanding of those even closest to Him was often less than stellar. Having witnessed or heard accounts of His previous miracles, His brothers urged Him to go publicly to Judea and gain the recognition they thought He desired. In Judea, the Feast of Booths, also known as the Festival of Tabernacles, which would draw crowds of religious leaders and laypeople from surrounding areas, was about to rev up. To the practical eye, this would seem the precise moment to gain public recognition. Yet Christ had no interest in gaining attention; His interest was in fulfilling His commission from God.

Read aloud John 7:1–5. What impression about Jesus's brothers do you get from the advice they gave?

After these things Jesus was walking in Galilee, for He was unwilling to walk in Judea because the Jews were seeking to kill Him. Now the feast of the Jews, the Feast of Booths, was near. Therefore His brothers said to Him, "Leave here and go into Judea, so that Your disciples also may see Your works which You are doing. For no one does anything in secret when he himself seeks to be known publicly. If You do these things, show Yourself to the world." For not even His brothers were believing in Him.
—John 7:1–5

The source of the advice Jesus's brothers gave Him is fairly obvious: disbelief. I can hear them now: "Go on to Judea and do the same miracles you have been doing elsewhere. After all, attention is what you are really after, right? If attention is what you want, attention is definitely what you will get there" (author's paraphrase). You can almost hear the sarcasm dripping off their words. They were not simply suggesting that Jesus share His message with a common group of people; they wanted Him to expose Himself at a religious festival, which was a place where supposed idolatry and blasphemy would not be tolerated.

Not falling prey to their cunning comments, Jesus reminded His brothers that His time had not yet arrived. However, their time was always at hand, *"always opportune"* (v. 6). He stated that the world hated Him, while assuring them that they would not be hated.

 Compare John 7:6–7 with John 15:18–19. Describe the reason stated in these verses as to why someone would not be hated by the world but rather loved by it.

So Jesus said to them, "My time is not yet here, but your time is always opportune. The world cannot hate you, but it hates Me because I testify of it, that its deeds are evil."
—John 7:6–7

"If the world hates you, you know that it has hated Me before it hated you. If you were of the world, the world would love its own; but because you are not of the world, but I chose you out of the world, because of this the world hates you."
—John 15:18–19

Contrary to what one would assume, being told by Christ that the *"world cannot hate you"* is not a comforting message! The verses you just read remind us that when we become children of God, we are, in essence, called to be set apart from the world. Our lives and testimonies should point to Him and, as a result, speak a message of conviction. Those who deny Christ will be embraced by the world for they do not tend to speak or act in a way that removes the blinding shades of sin-filled comfort.

After Jesus allowed His brothers to leave without Him for the festival, He too made His way to Jerusalem. However, He did so secretly. His reputation preceded Him, for the Jerusalem leaders were looking for Him. Among the crowds were great disputes, as people wondered, *Who is this Jesus?*

There was much grumbling among the crowds concerning Him; some were saying, "He is a good man"; others were saying, "No, on the contrary, He leads the people astray."
—John 7:12

 Identify and discuss two labels given to Christ by the crowds.

Do these labels—*good man* and *deceiver*—sound familiar? The same arguments heard today concerning the identity of Christ were being discussed centuries ago! Some people in the crowds were saying He was a good man; others in the crowds were saying He was deceiving people.

The concept of Jesus being simply a good man is a current popular thought. Modern society tells us that it is not just OK but even admirable to be good, to be spiritual. Discussion about the latest spiritual trend crops up everywhere—from TV talk shows to grocery store lines. *God,* when spoken of generically, is also widely accepted. After the tragedy on September 11, 2001, believing in God almost became cliché. However, when the name *Jesus Christ* is introduced into a conversation, the discussion suddenly takes a sharp turn and often meets a wall.

Considering Jesus to be a deceiver or someone who *"leads the people astray"* (John 7:12) is a convenient, yet sadly useless, balm to sooth a convicted soul. Some people grasp this idea quickly. Why? Because if Jesus Christ set out to deceive people, then it is honorable to not only deny but detest His teachings.

Satan is so cunning. He has used many of the same arguments against the true belief in Christ all throughout history, and yet many people still fall into his preset traps of thinking of Jesus Christ in false ways—for example, as just a good man or a deceiver. Without a proper understanding of who Christ is through the study of the Scriptures, each of us walks dangerously close to the edge of Satan's deception.

While people were debating over the identity of Jesus, He walked into the Temple and began to teach. Notice that it was His teaching that gained the attention of the higher-ups. They began remarking to one another about the power and authority with which He taught; yet according to their understanding, He had not been trained or educated (v. 15). I can only imagine what Christ must have sounded like when speaking the very words that spoke of Him! He was the fulfillment of the Scriptures yet was unidentified by the crowd because He did not fit their preconceived ideas.

 Identify any concepts of Christ you have held in the past that do not fit your new understanding of Him gained through the study of the Scriptures.

Jesus replied to the questioning crowd by saying, *"My teaching is not Mine, but His who sent Me"* (John 7:16). Jesus immediately deflected any praise for His teaching from being solely on Him and pointed toward His Father as the authority. He then associated one's willingness to do God's will with one's ability to discern the authenticity of His (Jesus's) teaching:

"If anyone is willing to do His will, he will know of the teaching, whether it is of God or whether I speak from Myself."
—John 7:17

According to Jesus Christ's statement, if you want to do God's will, you will recognize Jesus's teachings as being from God. To know God's will, we need to listen to His Son. God, in His sovereignty and wisdom, has chosen to make all things known through His Son, Jesus Christ. Should we choose to deny Christ, we deny God.

Confused, some of the people in the crowd began to murmur, *"Is this not the man whom they are seeking to kill?"* (John 7:25). They had heard reports that this man was being sought after by the local officials, and there He was, standing in a public place speaking freely. Questions and comments, therefore, began to arise and trickle through the crowd: "Do the authorities think that He is the Messiah?" "No way! We know where He came from."

 How did Jesus respond to these comments?

Then Jesus cried out in the temple, teaching and saying, "You both know Me and know where I am from; and I have not come of Myself, but He who sent Me is true, whom you do not know. I know Him, because I am from Him, and He sent Me."
—John 7:28–29

The Scriptures leave no room for confusion on this issue: Christ repeatedly claimed to have been sent from God and to know God. These two claims filled the officials with rage. Therefore, they tried once more to seize Him, yet He evaded their grasp again *"because His hour had not yet come"* (John 7:30).

John 7:37–53

In the first few verses of this section, Christ again made a public statement that created conflict and division.

Now on the last day, the great day of the feast, Jesus stood and cried out, saying, "If anyone is thirsty, let him come to Me and drink. He

who believes in Me, as the Scripture said, 'From his innermost being will flow rivers of living water.' "
—John 7:37–38

Discuss the analogy Christ used in the preceding passage.

On the last and most important day of the Jewish festival, Jesus stood up and proclaimed that belief in Him would provide "rivers" of spiritual refreshment. In this announcement, He was making a bold public profession of deity. Within Him is the source of all completeness. Belief in Him would be followed by an indwelling of the Holy Spirit, who was to come after Jesus's resurrection from the dead.

Because of Jesus Christ's bold words, division occurred once again. Some believed; others attached false labels; all were affected. His attraction caused some to want to seize Him; yet again, He eluded capture. Christ was, in essence, untouchable until God said, "You may seize Him."

Have you ever considered the fact that Jesus Christ was invincible until He allowed Himself to be handed over to authorities at the time appointed by His Father? How does this truth encourage or challenge your answer to the question, Who is this Jesus?

Personal Reflection

1. **Have I ever fully understood Jesus's claim that His teaching comes directly from God (John 7:16–17)? If so, how does this affect the way I read and implement the Scriptures?**

2. **How do my daily actions display my own belief in Christ?**

The Word in the World

Honey, Where Are Your Accusers?

When invited to come to Jesus for salvation, people often offer the excuse, "I would come to Jesus, but I'm just not ready." The same people sometimes try to justify that excuse, saying, "If only you knew what I've done in my life." Several versions of this response have been given to me when I've attempted to share Christ with friends and others. The reality is that not one of us is ever ready to come to Christ. Remember, Romans 3:23 states that we all have sinned and fallen short. We all are in the same situation: desperately in need of salvation through Jesus Christ.

If you already know Christ, I challenge you to reflect on your personal state of desperation for His grace in your life and in what ways He has cleansed you and freed you from past sins. Perhaps you need to offer love and acceptance in the name of Christ to certain people in your life and drop any stones you have considered throwing (John 8:3-11).

If you do not know Christ as your Savior, let me be the first one to say to you, "Honey, where are your accusers?" None of us have the right to condemn you. We can, however, offer you the hope and grace we have found in Jesus Christ. Let today be the first day of your walk with Christ as your personal Savior.

Week 8  John 8

The Truth Will Set You Free

So Jesus said to the Jews who had believed Him, "If you continue in My word, you really are My disciples. You will know the truth, and the truth will set you free."
—John 8:31–32 (HCSB)

John 8:1–20

No one enjoys being accused of wrongdoing. Being disciplined, even by someone who loves us, is tough to handle. A private confrontation is bad enough, but public ridicule is often more than we can shoulder. Imagine being thrown in front of a crowd of finger-pointing strangers who want only to catch someone else in a trap. John records one such incident near the beginning of chapter 8:

Early in the morning [Jesus] came again into the temple, and all the people were coming to Him; and He sat down and began to teach them. The scribes and the Pharisees brought a woman caught in adultery, and having set her in the center of the court, they said to Him, "Teacher, this woman has been caught in adultery, in the very act. Now in the Law Moses commanded us to stone such women; what then do You say?" They were saying this, testing Him, so that they might have grounds for accusing Him. But Jesus stooped down and with His finger wrote on the ground.
—John 8:2–6

Read aloud the preceding passage and answer these questions:

• For what sin was the woman brought before Christ?

• What was the true intent of the Pharisees?

We find Christ seated in the temple complex, teaching those who had drawn near. Then came a sudden interruption. A crowd of scribes and Pharisees dragged in an assuredly ashamed woman and set her before the unsuspecting audience. Before anyone had time to ask questions, the nature of her crime was announced—*adultery.*

Pharisees and scribes were teachers and translators of the law. They were well versed in Old Testament Scriptures, for this was their life and job. In an attempt to corner Jesus into contradicting the law, these Pharisees and scribes had brought to Him a person caught in the act of a sin that, according to the Mosaic Law, demanded harsh punishment—death.

 According to the following verse, what was the Jewish law concerning those caught in adultery?

If there is a man who commits adultery with another man's wife, one who commits adultery with his friend's wife, the adulterer and the adulteress shall surely be put to death.
—Leviticus 20:10

The Pharisees presented Jesus with quite a test! They knew that Jewish law demanded that this woman be put to death. Public stoning would have been the most likely means of death. Each participant would hurl rocks at the accused until he or she succumbed to death. Yet note who was missing from this public display. Her partner! The Mosaic Law demanded that both partners involved in the affair be put to death. The absence of the man hints at the true intention of this interruption. Had the Pharisees truly been interested in seeking justice, they would have followed the letter of the law. Instead, they were merely seeking an excuse to place Jesus on the *hot seat,* for lack of a better term.

If they could catch Jesus Christ speaking a verdict that went against their law, they would have grounds for accusing Him. They might have been boasting to themselves about the assured success of this trap. But Jesus unexpectedly bent down and began to write on the ground. Amidst persistent questioning, He continued to write. Although we are not told what He wrote on the ground, we are given the final instruction He declared before the accusers.

Write the command Christ gave to the accusers in John 8:7.

Whatever those divine fingers sketched in the dirt, Jesus's response was powerful enough to cause each person, one by one, to turn and walk away. I am so thankful that God is not amused by our public humiliation. Rather, He deals with our sin individually, while reminding others that they, too, have discrepancies of their own. Before He will allow our demise by the hands of fellow sinners, He offers His own in forgiveness.

When left alone with the woman, Jesus extended grace and two simple commands:

> *Straightening up, Jesus said to her, "Woman, where are they? Did no one condemn you?" She said, "No one, Lord." And Jesus said, "I do not condemn you, either. Go. From now on sin no more."*
> —John 8:10–11

Read aloud the previous verses. Describe how Christ demonstrated grace, and write out the commands He gave the woman.

Notice that the Pharisees had not walked away too far because they heard Jesus when He spoke again to *"them,"* saying, *"I am the Light of the world; he who follows Me will not walk in the darkness, but will have the Light of life"* (John 8:12). They may have dropped their stones, but anger was still balled up in their hands. They declared His testimony *"not true,"* because according to the Law of Moses, at least two witnesses are required to make any legal claim true.

Read John 8:14–20 in your Bible, then describe Jesus's response to the accusation about the need for two witnesses.

"Even in your law it has been written that the testimony of two men is true. I am He who testifies about Myself, and the Father who sent Me testifies about Me."
—John 8:17–18

Christ reinforced His stance that He is directed and sent by His Father (God). God is His validation! What other witness does one need? Less than amused, the Pharisees asked, *"Where is Your Father?"* (v. 19). Displaying their lack of understanding of God as Father, they looked to the obvious. Christ asserted that those who know Him know His Father also.

> *So they were saying to Him, "Where is Your Father?" Jesus answered, "You know neither Me nor My Father; if you knew Me, you would know My Father also."*
> —John 8:19

 How does Christ's statement in John 8:19 associate knowledge of Him with knowledge of the Father?

John 8:21–59

The Pharisees' confusion deepened when Jesus spoke of His upcoming departure. He predicted that He was about to go somewhere they would never find. There is an important caution in His warning.

> *Then He said again to them, "I go away, and you will seek Me, and will die in your sin; where I am going, you cannot come." So the Jews were saying, "Surely He will not kill Himself, will He, since He says, 'Where I am going, you cannot come'?" And He was saying to them, "You are from below, I am from above; you are of this world, I am not of this world. Therefore I said to you that you will die in your sins; for unless you believe that I am He, you will die in your sins."*
> —John 8:21–24

Read the previous passage aloud. What caution are we given? In whom must we place our faith in order to avoid dying in our sin?

Jesus told the Pharisees that unless they placed their faith in Him and His teaching, they would most assuredly die in their sins. This statement rings true for all of us even today. Having faith is not enough. In whom our faith is grounded is of utmost importance. Apart from Christ, we are in bondage to our sin. He alone is the key to our freedom.

This was a radical proclamation! The Pharisees therefore stared at Him and said, *"Who are You?"* (v. 25). This Man, who had been gaining attention for performing various miracles, had been teaching with unknown authority in the Temple, and had just finished writing convicting messages in the dirt, was conversing with the religious lawgivers of the time essentially saying, "I'm the Son of God; believe in Me, or die in your sins." Admittedly, Christ was not the exact picture of salvation the Pharisees were looking for. But the decision had to be made: stubbornly hang on to their preconceived ideas of what Christ ought to look like or step out in faith and obedience to the Man speaking before them.

 Have you ever struggled with destroying your own false conceptions of Christ in order to align your belief with the Scriptures? If so, how?

Scripture tells us that some in the crowd overheard this conversation and placed their faith in Jesus Christ. When Christ spoke, decisions were made. Once given the opportunity to believe in Him, those who heard His message stood equally accountable for their decisions.

 How does John 3:16–18 relate to the accountability of those who refuse to place their faith in Christ?

"For God so loved the world, that He gave His only begotten Son, that whoever believes in Him shall not perish, but have eternal life. For

God did not send the Son into the world to judge the world, but that the world might be saved through Him. He who believes in Him is not judged; he who does not believe has been judged already, because he has not believed in the name of the only begotten Son of God."
—John 3:16–18

It is a fearful thing for persons to have heard the message of Christ and then turned their backs. In that turning, they find themselves facing condemnation, judgment, and eternity apart from the immediate presence of God. This decision far outweighs all other choices in life. Refusing faith in Jesus Christ is actually choosing eternal damnation.

Thankfully, however, clear hope and joy are available for those of us who have placed our faith in Jesus Christ for salvation. The Scriptures even give us road signs along life's journey to ensure we are going in the right direction.

 List three promises given to believers in the following passage.

So Jesus said to the Jews who had believed Him, "If you continue in My word, you really are My disciples. You will know the truth, and the truth will set you free."
—John 8:31–32 (HCSB)

After Jesus Christ had spoken to those who rejected Him and His words, He turned toward the others who placed their faith in Him, and He gave them three promises, which apply also to those of us who are believers today. First, we can have assurance that we are truly His disciples if we continue in His Word. As we come to know Christ, we desire to know and dig into His Word, the Scriptures. The very fact that we have a passion to know God's Word and apply it to our lives points mightily to the fact that we are disciples of Christ. Secondly, if we remain in God's Word, we will *"know the truth."* The Scriptures will lead us into truth. The Scriptures, by their very nature, cannot lead us elsewhere. We have bold assurance in knowing that if we remain in God's Word, it will show us truth. And lastly, truth will set us free. Do you see the sequence of events here? We remain in God's Word. God's Word leads us to truth. Truth sets us free. It sounds simple, yet we risk missing out on these promises if we fail to *remain* in the Word.

Discuss the significance of remaining in God's Word and how this action affects our reception of the associated promises.

The people in the crowd who chose not to believe in Jesus Christ and objected to some of the things He was saying began to reference their relationship with Abraham, primary patriarch of the Jewish faith: *"Abraham is our father"* (John 8:39). Rather than deal with the present reality of Christ appearing before them, they chose, instead, to base their security in their ancestry. Abraham was a man of mighty faith in God and, through God's promise to him, became the father of nations. (See Genesis 12:1–3.) What these people were missing, however, was their renowned ancestor's *faith.*

 In what ways have you relied upon the faith of someone else rather than your own?

Being a part of Abraham's family tree was not impressive to Christ. He was much more interested in each person's object of faith. Where we place our personal faith is of far more importance than from whom we get our beautiful eyes.

Christ turned these Jews' own argument against them by saying, *"If you are Abraham's children, do the deeds of Abraham"* (John 8:39). Abraham had placed His faith in God, but when the Son of God appeared on the scene, "Abraham's kids" squinted their eyes and dared to doubt Him! Instead of celebrating their tie to a genetic father, Christ pointed out that those who deny Him share a far more sinister "parent"—the devil (v. 44).

 Read aloud the following passage. What reason did Jesus give for those who refused to listen to and believe in Him?

Jesus said to them, "If God were your Father, you would love Me, for I proceeded forth and have come from God, for I have not even come on My own initiative, but He sent Me. Why do you not understand what

I am saying? It is because you cannot hear My word. You are of your father the devil, and you want to do the desires of your father. He was a murderer from the beginning, and does not stand in the truth because there is no truth in him. Whenever he speaks a lie, he speaks from his own nature, for he is a liar and the father of lies. But because I speak the truth, you do not believe Me. Which one of you convicts Me of sin? If I speak truth, why do you not believe Me? He who is of God hears the words of God; for this reason you do not hear them, because you are not of God."
—John 8:42–47

 List all the qualities of the devil revealed in the previous passage.

The John 8:42–47 passage does not speak of the devil as a mythological or imaginary creature. His existence is spoken of in fact, and a list of his distasteful characteristics is there for us to read. Mark his character; memorize the stench of his presence. Persistent disbelief of God, distaste for His Son, and hatred for His Holy Word are earmarks of Satan's influence.

The ranting against Christ picks up again in verse 48 and continues on and off through verse 59. Many people, when convicted, respond with accusations against the accuser rather than immediate repentance and faith. I cannot help but believe this is what the people being quoted at the end of John 8 were doing. After all, the Son of God was speaking directly to them. They were hearing straight from His lips the words we read in the Scriptures. If such words convict us through the written route, how much more must they have convicted through direct proclamation!

Jesus concluded the discussion by claiming to have seen and known Abraham. Knowing this to be physically impossible due to the time factor, His hearers questioned this claim.

 Write out what Jesus said about His temporal relationship to Abraham (v. 58).

How does Jesus's response compare with what you have learned about Him from John 1:1–3?

In the beginning was the Word, and the Word was with God, and the Word was God. He was in the beginning with God. All things came into being through Him, and apart from Him nothing came into being that has come into being.
—John 1:1–3

I love to see Scripture confirm Scripture and build on our prior knowledge! Christ's statement in John 8:58 reminds us that He has always existed. Consider these facts: Before Christ was born on earth, He had existed from all eternity. He is God. He is timeless. He offers forgiveness, truth, and freedom. And He demands faith, trust, and obedience.

Personal Reflection

1. **How would I have reacted if my private sins had been made public in the way described in this eighth chapter of John?**

2. **Has this chapter challenged my understanding of the devil's influence in my life and the lives of others? If so, how?**

The Word in the World

The Deceiver and the Seeker: Truth Does Exist

This past summer, I spent most of my evenings writing this book. So I treated myself from time to time by taking my laptop to the local mega bookstore to enjoy the coffee and atmosphere while I wrote.

One day two guys sat down beside me, and it was noticeable through the conversation that one guy, whom I have dubbed "the deceiver," was trying to convince the other guy, "the seeker," to believe that it is not important what you believe in life as long as you are happy. This drove me wild, so I started to pray: "Lord, you know I want to be involved in that conversation. Please open a door for me to talk with them."

Shortly afterwards, the deceiver got up to get coffee. I leaned over to the other guy, the seeker, and initiated conversation: "Excuse me, but I could not help overhearing you talk about your faith, and you mentioned Kabala.* Is this what you practice?"

"Oh, no," he replied. "I have studied it, but something about it doesn't feel right to me."

"I would encourage you to go with that feeling," I responded. "The reason it doesn't feel right is because it is not truth. If you want truth, read the Bible."

The deceiver returned and was less than happy to see me speaking with his target.

*Kabala, according to *Merriam-Webster's Online Dictionary*, is a medieval and modern system of Jewish theosophy, mysticism, and thaumaturgy marked by belief in creation through emanation and a cipher method of interpreting Scripture.

Once I Was Blind

A blind man
The blind man's parents

He then answered, "Whether [the Man who healed me] is a sinner, I do not know; one thing I do know, that though I was blind, now I see."
—John 9:25

John 9:1–12

This description of Jesus healing a blind man is one of my favorite accounts in the Book of John. Every time I read this chapter, I fall in love with the man who once was blind. Although he did not possess the luxury of sight his entire life, he definitely was well equipped in speaking his mind! Through this chapter, we are privy to several occasions in which he boldly spoke truth the way he "saw" it, despite the disbelief or even ridicule of others. Even when the healed man did not know his Healer in His fullness, he did not shy away from his honest testimony. When he later discovered the identity of Christ (who actually called Himself the Son of Man), his new sight proved very keen, because he immediately accepted Him as Lord and worshipped Him.

According to John 9:1–3, for what reason was this man born blind?

As He passed by, He saw a man blind from birth. And His disciples asked Him, "Rabbi, who sinned, this man or his parents, that he would be born blind?" Jesus answered, "It was neither that this man

sinned, nor his parents; but it was so that the works of God might be
displayed in him."
—John 9:1–3

I find it amazing that God uses even our disabilities to glorify Him. Rejecting the optional reasons the disciples offered for the man's blindness, Christ told them that the blindness was not a result of sin; rather, the condition had happened so that God's work might be displayed in this man. Although not all of us will be healed from our physical imperfections while on earth, I do believe that every aspect of our lives provides opportunity for the glory of God to be displayed.

 List some aspects of your life that you have never before considered to be potential routes of bringing glory to God.

I am so thankful that God does not demand perfection, but rather provides it! If He listened only to those who sing perfectly in tune, I would be blacklisted from worship services. Thankfully, however, He takes what we have to offer and creates masterpieces that could be crafted only by His hands. He saw such a masterpiece in this man born blind.

 What was the man instructed to do in order to receive his sight (vv. 6–7)?

When [Jesus] had said this, He spat on the ground, and made clay
of the spittle, and applied the clay to his eyes, and said to him, "Go,
wash in the pool of Siloam" (which is translated, Sent). So he went
away and washed, and came back seeing.
—John 9:6–7

This act was of no *little* faith; it was an early illustration of the blind man's willingness to be obedient and trusting. Think about it. Someone he had never known just walked up to him, spit on the ground to make clay, smeared the clay all over his eyes, and said, *"Go, wash in the pool of Siloam"* (v. 7). Instead of angrily knocking the mud off with his hands and feeling insulted, the man did as he was instructed. He left blind and maybe a little perplexed at the request, but he came back with sight! His act of obedience brought him sight.

 Can you think of some areas in your life that could use some spiritual "mud packs"? If so, what is keeping you from believing that God can and will use any area of weakness in your life to glorify Himself?

The newly acquired vision of the man born blind quickly gained him notoriety. Is it not true that when God heals us from something, people may not always be quick to give Him the credit, but they will certainly wonder what happened?

The first ones to notice the blind man had gained his sight were his neighbors. I can hear them now: "Huh? Well, he looks like our blind neighbor, but certainly must not be. That poor guy has been blind since birth." Others were not so quick to dismiss the possibility. All the while, he spoke up and spoke truth.

 What was the healed man's response to the questions surrounding his identity (v. 9)?

Despite the confusion of others, the man clearly spoke up and identified himself, proclaiming, *"I am the one"* (v. 9). This obviously led to more questions. How could this man, whom they all knew had grown up blind, suddenly have sight? He voiced his testimony of what had taken place, simple as it was, yet amazingly complex.

 Write the man's testimony (v. 11).

I am convicted by the fact that man born blind shared with others exactly how the event happened. A miraculous change occurred in his life through something as ordinary as mud. We may sometimes feel our testimonies are a little plain. Maybe we were never delivered from a major addiction or lived a life that made headlines, but every story of a life changed by God holds the potential of greatness.

John 9:13–34

Apparently the news of this man's healing spread, because he was soon brought before the Pharisees. As we have seen already throughout the Scriptures, the Pharisees, though disbelieving, could not resist wanting to find out more about this Man named Jesus. Jesus Christ had already confused them through His healing of the sick man at the Pool of Bethesda, teachings in the Temple, and forgiveness of the adulterous woman. So they were eager to come up with their next accusation against Jesus.

 Compare what you learned in John 5:8–10 with the information you are given in John 9:14. Why would the fact that these healings took place on the Sabbath be of special interest to the Pharisees?

Jesus said to him, "Get up, pick up your pallet and walk." Immediately the man became well, and picked up his pallet and began to walk. Now it was the Sabbath on that day. So the Jews were saying to the man who was cured, "It is the Sabbath, and it is not permissible for you to carry your pallet."
—John 5:8–10

Now it was a Sabbath on the day when Jesus made the clay and opened his eyes.
—John 9:14

The one who received his sight had obviously been instructed in the Jewish law. We can confidently assume that he was aware of the laws concerning the Sabbath. However, even when brought before the lawgivers and officials and questioned about his alleged healing, he did not waver in his testimony.

Although seemingly simple, his testimony caused division. Some argued that Jesus could not be from God because He had healed on the Sabbath. Others argued that a sinful man would not be able to perform such signs. The healed man did not have to elaborate his story to cause conviction or division. The power of our testimonies is not in our rendition or concoction of great events but rather in our straightforward sharing of simple truth.

We next see my beloved hero standing strong even when his parents cracked under the pressure. His parents had been summoned because the Jews still did not believe the man had been born blind. When questioned before the lawgivers, his parents spoke the simple truth, but were careful to add nothing more. Basically, they admitted, "Oh, he is our son all right. He was born blind, but we are not sure what happened. Besides, he is old enough now to speak for himself."

What was the reason for the parents' desire for their son to speak for himself (vv. 22–23)?

His parents said this because they were afraid of the Jews; for the Jews had already agreed that if anyone confessed Him to be Christ, he was to be put out of the synagogue. For this reason his parents said, "He is of age; ask him."
—John 9:22–23

The parents' response brings to mind that old adage, "Every man for himself." Even the mom and dad were not willing to place their necks on the line for their son's testimony. Agreeing with him could have resulted in being kicked out of the synagogue, which was their place of meeting and worship.

So, once more, the Pharisees called in the healed man, where, for the third time, he shared his testimony. Not being sure of the exact nature of Jesus Christ, the man summed up his story in one short profound statement.

Write the healed man's testimony, as found in John 9:25.

No elaboration; just a simplistic and strong statement. Frustrated by his antagonists' persistent questioning, he finally said, *"I told you already and you did not listen; why do you want to hear it again? You do not want to become His disciples too, do you?"* (John 9:27). These interrogators objected strongly to the healed man's last question and reviled him, but he did not wither in their presence. Rather, he came back with very pointed remarks. In response, they became very defensive and threw him out.

John 9:35–38

When we stand up for truth, the world may not always appreciate our honesty, but Christ does. When Jesus heard that the healed man had been thrown out, He found him and asked him this question: *"Do you believe in the Son of Man?"* (v. 35). When the man responded with a desire to believe, Christ revealed His identity to him.

> *Jesus heard that they had put him out, and finding him, He said, "Do you believe in the Son of Man?" He answered, "Who is He, Lord, that I may believe in Him?" Jesus said to him, "You have both seen Him, and He is the one who is talking with you." And he said, "Lord, I believe." And he worshiped Him.*
> —John 9:35–38

 How did the healed man respond to Christ's revelation of Himself as the Son of Man (v. 38)?

Scripture records that the man immediately believed in Christ and subsequently began to worship Him. What an important picture! True faith, whether new or weathered, ought to result in worship. When we come to the realization that Jesus Christ came into the world, died for our sins, and offered Himself as the assurance of our eternal salvation, worship is sure to follow.

John 9:39–41

After Jesus revealed Himself to the man born blind, He began explaining His reason for coming to this world.

> *And Jesus said, "For judgment I came into this world, so that those who do not see may see, and that those who see may become blind."*
> —John 9:39

 Discuss the statement of purpose Christ offered (v. 39).

Using an analogy once more, Christ said that He came into the world to give sight to the blind as well as to blind the eyes of those who see. Just as Christ provided physical sight for this man born blind, He desires to grant spiritual sight to all who place their faith in Him. Our spiritual eyes are born naturally closed due to sin. When we reach out and trust Him for our salvation and forgiveness of sin, He miraculously opens those eyes. This sight, however, is available only to those who have a personal relationship with Him. Though our physical vision may be 20/20, we are spiritually blind if we have never given our lives to Jesus Christ.

Personal Reflection

1. **In what ways have I acted like the blind man's parents by refusing to step up and say what I believe in fear that I may get "kicked out" of some relationships or opportunities in life?**

2. **If I am honest with myself, which one of the following statements best describes my current state of spiritual sight?**
   - ❑ **I am spiritually blind.**
   - ❑ **I desire to know more about Jesus Christ; I want to see.**
   - ❑ **I once was blind, but now I see through faith in Jesus Christ.**

3. **If I confess to having "seen" Christ, does my life reflect a lifestyle of worship? If not, what is currently blinding me to His presence?**

The Word in the World

Gena: You Can Lead Me to the Door

Gena is a co-worker of mine who began asking me questions about God after I offered to pray for her once while she was taking college exams. This offer sparked several more conversations that always rotated around who Christ claimed to be. Our conversations continued for over a year and a half, each slowly building on her understanding of who God is.

One day she finally said, "Lorie, I feel like you can lead me to the door, but I have to make the decision to walk through." On March 25, 2004, Gena and I met at a local coffee shop to once again walk through the Scriptures together. That day, she shared how she felt "disconnected from God." I was able to share the gospel with her and see her accept Christ as her Savior. She and her family are now attending church, and she is growing in her walk with God.

Week 10   John 10

I Am the Good Shepherd

People Introduced

No new people introduced

"I am the good shepherd; the good shepherd lays down His life for the sheep."
—John 10:11

John 10:1–6

Jesus used many illustrations to teach important lessons. Something about visual images helps us to remember a lesson long after the original words have been spoken. Such is the case in John 10:1–6. Christ knew that His audience was very familiar with the art of shepherding; therefore, He used an illustration they should have been able to understand well. Although most of us today have no personal experience with shepherding, we can still understand the message Jesus intended.

Draw a box to represent a sheep pen. Allow one side to have a small opening, and label the opening "door."

Historically, sheep pens had only one door. The walls served as protection and a means to keep the sheep herded together. Once the sheep were safe inside for the evening, the shepherd would lie down at the entrance, or door. Anything or anyone who wanted into the pen had to first go past the shepherd. This protective practice of the shepherd was extremely important because sheep are naturally fairly easy prey. They do not possess the means to defend themselves, nor are they known for being aggressive. Think about it: when was the last time you heard about a random sheep attack?

 Fill in the blanks below by referring to John 10:3:

"He calls his own sheep _____ _____ *and leads them out."*
—John 10:3

The shepherd knows His sheep so intimately that he calls them by name! The sheep do not respond to just anyone's voice. They know, or recognize, their master's voice and confidently follow him out of their safe haven and into open areas (v. 4). However, if confronted with an unfamiliar voice, they run (v. 5)! I love this. When the sheep do not recognize a voice, they do not sit around and debate the pros and cons about what it says; they head for the hills, or wherever else sheep go. We can learn a lot from sheep in regard to knowing our Master's voice and fleeing upon hearing the voice of a stranger.

John 10:7–21

Jesus noticed that His listeners did not understand His analogy, so He went on to explain that He is *"the door of the sheep"* (v. 7). Like sheep, we are in need of protection and guidance. Christ has come to lead and protect us, and He knows us each by name! Though others may attempt to scale the walls of our safe area to sneak into our lives to destroy us, Christ, having offered Himself as a sacrifice, provides protection for us.

 Draw a stick figure of a man at the door of sheep pen you drew. Write the John 10:9 verse near the door.

Christ explained that just as there is only one correct way to enter a sheep pen, there is only one way to enter into eternal salvation. He alone is the door. All those who try to enter through other means are imitators; they are thieves and robbers.

 List all the facts the following passage shows us about the Good Shepherd and the hired man.

"I am the good shepherd; the good shepherd lays down His life for the sheep. He who is a hired hand, and not a shepherd, who is not the

owner of the sheep, sees the wolf coming, and leaves the sheep and flees, and the wolf snatches them and scatters them. He flees because he is a hired hand and is not concerned about the sheep. I am the good shepherd, and I know My own and My own know Me, even as the Father knows Me and I know the Father; and I lay down My life for the sheep."
—John 10:11–15

Good Shepherd   **Hired Man**

The true shepherd will lay down his life for his sheep. When danger comes, the true shepherd will stay and risk his life to protect his sheep, unlike a hired man, who will run because he has no personal interest in the well-being of something that is not his own.

Christ called Himself *"the good shepherd."* Because He knows and loves us, He was willing to lay down His own life so that ours would be spared. And He did this willingly, without pressure or coercion.

 How does the following passage relate to what we have previously studied about Jesus awaiting His appointed time?

"For this reason the Father loves Me, because I lay down My life so that I may take it again. No one has taken it away from Me, but I lay it down on My own initiative. I have authority to lay it down, and I have authority to take it up again. This commandment I received from My Father."
—John 10:17–18

Don't miss this. Christ so loved us that He willingly laid down His life for us. Danger was coming our way: sin. All of us sin (Romans 3:23). Sin demands justice be paid, and that justice is death (Romans 6:23). Rather than leaving us alone in our sin, helpless and doomed, Christ paid the final price. We are left with having to make a choice: Will we follow imitators, who scale our walls of protection and lead us into destruction and death, or will we place our faith in Jesus Christ, who is the only true Door to salvation?

John 10:22–42

While walking in the temple complex in Jerusalem, Jesus became surrounded once more by Jews who wanted to ask Him questions. They demanded that He tell them plainly whether He was the Christ. Jesus responded by saying that He had shown them. The works that He had done testified to Him, yet they did not believe.

What reason is given for the Jews' disbelief (v. 26)?

Persons who know Jesus Christ as Savior and Lord—Christ's sheep—have certain distinguishing characteristics.

> *"My sheep hear My voice, and I know them, and they follow Me; and I give eternal life to them, and they will never perish; and no one will snatch them out of My hand. My Father, who has given them to Me, is greater than all; and no one is able to snatch them out of the Father's hand."*
> —John 10:27–29

List the promises to and characteristics of those who are Christ's sheep.

Look closely at the promise found in verse 29: *"No one is able to snatch them out of the Father's hand."* Wow! Consider this deeply. Once we have come to faith in Christ, we are His—permanently. Nothing or no one can ever snatch us out of God's hand. We are forever secure, settled snuggly into our Father's palm. Though life will seem crazy at times, we can rest in the assurance that Christ is sufficient not only to get us into God's hand but also to keep us there for eternity.

Discuss how this promise can affect your attitude during times of doubt and trouble.

Christ's words caused His enemies to want to stone Him. The only fault they could find with Him was that He claimed to be God. If this were not true, He would indeed have been guilty. But Christ *is* God. Therefore, though their carnal eyes could not see the truth, Christ remained innocent in His claim. Many held stones ready to strike Him for His alleged blasphemy, whereas others saw truth in His claims and placed their faith in Him. The line was and still is drawn between His sheep and the rest of the world. His sheep hear His voice. Do you?

 Have you ever come to know Jesus Christ as the Shepherd of your life? If so, how are you learning to hear His voice? If not, what is hindering you from making the decision to follow Him?

Personal Reflection

1. **How have I already seen Christ play the role of Shepherd in protecting me against dangerous foes in my life?**

2. **If I have not yet placed my faith in Christ, what more am I waiting for? Are the current shepherds in my life living up to the promises Jesus Christ has given to me?**

The **Word** in the World

Hurting Waitress: Take It to Jesus

My seminary class met at a local restaurant for dinner. Having placed our orders, we were sitting at the table enjoying a time of fellowship when our tall, blonde waitress, skillfully balancing three plates on her arm, brought the appetizers. My professor asked her if we could pray for her during our time of prayer. The young woman's eyes immediately began to mist up at this request. She graciously declined and left.

I sat there for a few minutes, poking at my spinach quesadilla; I could not stop thinking about her: *What had gone through her mind? What was the source of her tears?*

I excused myself from the table and made my way to the kitchen area. When I peeped into the kitchen, I could see her standing there waiting to receive our food. She turned and saw me. I motioned for her, and she came to where I was. Looking a little puzzled, she asked if I needed anything.

I apologized that we had made her cry. I explained that we only wanted to pray for her and asked if I could do so then.

She explained that she had just recently ended a four-year relationship with a guy and was hurting.

I asked her whether she knew Jesus Christ. She said that she had asked Him into her heart when she was eight but uttered her last prayer at the age of ten.

Referring to a short verse in the Gospel of John, *"Jesus wept"* (11:35), I pointed out that Jesus knows when we hurt and He hurts with us, and that He wants us to trust Him, even in our painful times.

Then we walked through the Scriptures regarding how to place our faith in Christ, and she said that she understood. I asked her if I could pray with her, and she nodded yes.

Lazarus, Arise!

People Introduced
Lazarus (a personal friend of Jesus)
Mary and Martha (Lazarus's sisters)
Thomas (a disciple [follower] of Jesus)

Jesus said to her, "I am the resurrection and the life; he who believes in Me will live even if he dies, and everyone who lives and believes in Me will never die. Do you believe this?"
—**John 11:25–26**

John 11:1–16

In the last chapter, we observed Jesus once again being sought after by His fellow countrymen who wanted to kill Him. And again, He had escaped and left Jerusalem and even Judea. No one could capture Christ against His will. His exit, however, was short-lived. He received news that His friend Lazarus, who lived in the town of Bethany in Judea, was ill. Two days later, Jesus determined to return to that area. He came willingly into the midst of those who hated Him in order to be with those He loved.

Though fully divine, Christ robed Himself in human flesh and, thus, felt natural emotions, such as pain, joy, disappointment, and even sorrow. His tear ducts were just as capable of overflowing when He wept as are yours and mine. And wept He did. We will see in this chapter that Jesus Christ's concern for His friends was not just superficial; He loved them deeply, even to the point of weeping when they were hurting.

What an incredible God we serve! Despite His majesty, He shares our pain. He does not turn away in disgust or demand that we return when we look more presentable; rather, He sits beside us in our messy situations and says, "Cry little one; I'm here with you and I'm not leaving."

 How does the understanding that Jesus Christ has fully felt the emotion of sorrow affect your willingness to go to Him in full abandonment with your problems?

The Scriptures tell us about three of Jesus's close friends—Mary, Martha, and Lazarus. This sibling trio shared meals and, undoubtedly, many moments of joy and laughter with our Lord. Yet John 11 gives an account of when they shared a time of great distress. Lazarus had fallen ill, and his sisters sent word to Jesus about him being sick (v. 3). Upon receiving the news, Jesus made a proclamation about the illness.

 Write the promise and the purpose given for this illness, as stated in John 11:4.

Does this sound familiar? Maybe the promise (*"This sickness is not to end in death"*) does not, but the purpose (God's glory) should! This purpose is similar to the one given in John 9:3 concerning the blind man. Again, the disastrous circumstance described resulted in the display of the glory of God. This larger truth helps us to better understand the choices Christ made.

 According to John 11:6, how long did Christ wait to leave after hearing the urgent news?

Christ waited two days! When we present an urgent request before the Lord, we typically desire an immediate response. Can you imagine the hand-wringing and worrying Mary and Martha endured? Let's be real: When something serious is going on in life, it is hard to wait—and how much more so in cases of life and death! Yet can it be that not all things we deem to be urgent are actually crises in the eyes of God? In the case of Lazarus's death, God had a purpose—and in His timing, it was revealed.

Pull Up a Chair

I cannot leave this section without pointing out the comments of the disciples, especially the comment Thomas made. Notice that when Christ announced His intention to return to Judea, the disciples questioned Him with a reminder: *"The Jews were just now seeking to stone You, and are You going there again?"* (John 11:8). Once Thomas was resigned to the fact that Jesus was, indeed, returning to Judea, this not-so-positive disciple responded, *"Let us also go, so that we may die with Him"* (v. 16). It is so refreshing to be reminded that even these great heroes of the faith were, at times, just as doubtful and strongheaded as you and I can sometimes be.

To be sure that the disciples fully understood the magnitude of the miracle to come, Jesus spoke clearly about the gravity of Lazarus's condition.

 According to John 11:14, what was Lazarus's condition?

Christ plainly told His disciples that Lazarus was not sleeping nor was He in a really deep coma, but rather he was dead.

John 11:17–44

By the time Jesus arrived in Bethany, Lazarus had already been entombed for four days. Unlike our modern form of burial—six feet under lots of dirt—people in this area historically buried their dead in stone tombs, which were carved out of the walls of rocks. The people wrapped their dead with linens, adding herbs and spices, and then laid the dead within the tomb, which they then sealed with a large stone, sometimes shaped like an oversized nickel.

 Draw an illustration of Lazarus's tomb.

Friends, neighbors, and loved ones were gathering around Mary and Martha to console them. I am sure that even then, the equivalents of casseroles and cakes were lined up in every grieving home. Despite the presence of many fellow grievers, Martha, when she heard that Jesus was on His way there, left them immediately to go out to meet Him.

Explain how Martha's statements to Jesus Christ reflected her understanding of His association with God.

Martha then said to Jesus, "Lord, if You had been here, my brother would not have died. Even now I know that whatever You ask of God, God will give You."
—John 11:21–22

Jesus responded to her by saying, *"Your brother will rise again"* (John 11:23).

Although Martha had just made this *huge* statement of faith in Jesus Christ's abilities and standing with God, she accepted Jesus's statement as applying to future promises of God. I can hear her breathlessly explain, "I know, Lord. All of us who have placed our faith in You will rise again at Your return."

Jesus tried to redirect her thoughts to the here-and-now benefits that belief in Him could provide:

Jesus said to her, "I am the resurrection and the life; he who believes in Me will live even if he dies, and everyone who lives and believes in Me will never die. Do you believe this?"
—John 11:25–26

To this, Martha simply acknowledged her belief that Jesus was the Christ, the Son of God, without addressing what Jesus actually said. (Sometimes the things God tries to share with us go right over our heads too.) She then left to go tell Mary that Jesus had come and was calling for her.

 Compare Martha's and Mary's initial encounters with Christ after their brother's death, and state any differences you note.

Martha then said to Jesus, "Lord, if You had been here, my brother would not have died. Even now I know that whatever You ask of God, God will give You."
—John 11:21–22

Therefore, when Mary came where Jesus was, she saw Him, and fell at His feet, saying to Him, "Lord, if You had been here, my brother would not have died."
—John 11:32

They both spoke to Jesus with extreme honesty, telling Him, *"If You had been here, my brother would not have died"* (John 11:21, 32). Yet Mary fell to the ground at her Master's feet and wept. Note this carefully. She had no fear in speaking her heart to her Master. She knew that He had the power to save her brother, but so far, she had not seen that fulfilled. So we find her weeping and pouring out her heart with tears of pain.

We can rest in the fact that God not only can take but also desires our honesty, even if it is painful. We do not serve a God who despises the broken, but One who delights in restoring that which is shattered.

 When was the last time you poured out your heart to God with tears of pain? Describe what you experienced.

John revealed to us a compassionate side of Christ that I long to fully understand (vv. 33–36). He heard Mary's heart; He saw her tears; and all the while, He never pushed her away. In seeing Mary's tears, along with the weeping of others with her, Jesus was *"deeply moved"* (v. 33). He did not stand stoic and watch her with an unsympathetic eye but was moved by her pain.

 Write out John 11:35.

Jesus was so moved by her pain that He shared in her weeping. Jesus, God of creation, wept with the one who came to Him hurting. Oh, the wonder!

Jesus Christ then went to the tomb and commanded, *"Remove the stone"* (John 11:39). Look back at your drawing. The purpose of the stone was to block the entrance of the tomb. Jesus commanded for it to be rolled away.

Martha, being rational, reminded Him, "Umm, Lord, my dead brother has been in there four days. He probably stinks by now" (author's paraphrase of v. 39*b*). I love it! I am relieved when others in the Scriptures are captured as being as nearsighted and rational as I often am!

Jesus stood at the open tomb and commanded, *"Lazarus, come forth"* (v. 43). Three words, one command, spoken by God in the form of the Son was all it took for the dead man to come back to life.

John 11:45–57

Many Jews who had come to visit and grieve with Mary were present when Jesus Christ called Lazarus forth.

What were the two responses of those who witnessed this miracle?

Therefore many of the Jews who came to Mary, and saw what He had done, believed in Him. But some of them went to the Pharisees and told them the things which Jesus had done.
—John 11:45–46

As always, some people will see Christ and believe; others will deny Him and run to cause trouble. The tattler's testimonies brought the issue of Christ before the Sanhedrin (local high court). Even there, the authorities debated about what to do with Him. They decided to seek His arrest so they might take His life.

People continue to seek ways to deal with the matter of Christ. Some choose to try to hush those who speak of Him, threaten punishment for the use of His name, and create laws that forbid the worship of God. All the while, they cannot contain, quench, or eliminate the reality of Christ.

Just as Christ commanded Lazarus to *"come forth"* or to arise, each of us is given the opportunity to heed this command. Life is found in Christ. We start off dead in our sins, figuratively in our own tombs of stone, until we too hear His voice, believe, and arise.

Personal Reflection

1. **Has there ever been a time in my life when I felt like Lazarus? What "sicknesses" have overtaken me that God ultimately used for His own glory and good?**

2. **Do I trust God even when He feels distant? Mary fell at the feet of Christ, saying, "If you had been here." Do I understand the amazing reality that Christ is always here with me?**

The Word in the World

Melissa: The Point Is That I Am Crying

After attempting suicide, Melissa was admitted to the emergency room. When I stepped into the room to draw her blood, she turned her face from me. I said a silent prayer and began to ask her about her life. Noticing several scars on her arm from previous attempts, I asked if she had ever heard of Christ. I explained the gospel and asked if she understood.

She replied that she did not believe that she could go to heaven.

I told her that if she was not sure where she is going, she needed to stop making these attempts at her life because hell is not a place you can arrive at and decide you want to leave. Not sure whether she was listening, I gathered my belongings and left the room.

Shortly afterwards, she pushed the call button, signaling me at the desk. I arrived in her room to find her crying.

"Thank you for talking with me," she said. "I know that it did not look like I was listening, but I heard every word you said. You know, I have been in hospitals before, and I've heard people saying, 'Oh, she is only crying wolf.' Yet people need to understand that, yes, maybe I am crying wolf, but the point is that I am crying."

I prayed with her that God would grant her the faith to believe.

Week 12 🍵 John 12

Death Is Required for Increase

People Introduced
No new people introduced

> *"Truly, truly, I say to you, unless a grain of wheat falls into the earth and dies, it remains alone; but if it dies, it bears much fruit."*
> —John 12:24

John 12:1–8

Picture the scene with me: Jesus had returned to the home of the sibling trio that we studied about in chapter 11. Jesus was eating a home-cooked meal with people who had recently witnessed a major miracle. Lazarus, reclining at the table with Him, had tasted death and now, raised from the dead, tasted food again. Amazing! I trust I am not the only one who finds this combination of the normal and supernatural intriguing—enjoying a meal with friends, including a person raised from the dead! But such is par for the course with Christ.

In the midst of this scene, we find one sister, Mary, humbly positioned at the feet of Jesus Christ. There, she did something that was anything but normal. She brought a pound of fragrant oil, poured it on His feet, and proceeded to wipe His feet with her hair. It is important for us to grasp the concept of this act. This was no ordinary cooking oil. Rather, this was expensive oil that could have been set aside as a means of savings and security. Unlike today when our means are often secured in bank accounts, during Jesus's time on earth, people's means were often secured in their possessions. This oil, being worth almost a year's wages, was one of Mary's most expensive possessions. In other words, each drop of oil that trickled over her Savior's feet represented the pouring out of her deepest treasures at His feet. This public exhibit of outrageous, extravagant abandonment caught the attention of someone else in the room.

But Judas Iscariot, one of His disciples, who was intending to betray Him, said, "Why was this perfume not sold for three hundred denarii and given to poor people?"
—John 12:4–5

 How did Judas Iscariot respond to Mary's sacrifice?

Right in the middle of Mary's act of worship, while her hair was still damp from wiping her Savior's feet, Judas ridiculed Mary for her action. Judas immediately asked why the fragrant oil was not sold and the money given to the poor. This response sounds so spiritual, does it not? After all, giving to the poor is important. However, Judas was not really concerned about the poor; instead, he felt his own pockets had been robbed.

 According to the following verse, what was the true reason Judas was upset?

Now he said this, not because he was concerned about the poor, but because he was a thief, and as he had the money box, he used to pilfer what was put into it.
—John 12:6

Judas held on to the money purse. When he saw the event taking place, he did not see a loving act of sacrifice and worship. Instead, to him, this was a shameful waste of money.

 Can you relate to Mary? Has anyone ever misunderstood one of your acts of worship toward Christ? If so, describe the situation.

I love the next verse because it reminds me that Jesus will come to our defense. Upon hearing Judas's rebuke, Jesus replied, *"Let her alone"* (John 12:7). We are not told whether Mary heard this remark. The fact remains that Jesus heard her accuser and confronted him. When we seek to pour our offerings at Christ's feet, other people may accuse us of being impractical or silly. Some of their responses may sound outright hateful, whereas others, like the response of Judas, may make a spiritual-sounding argument against our action. Regardless of the comments, we can rest assured that Christ hears them and will come to our defense, even if our ears never hear the rebuke.

John 12:9–19

The fellowship time Jesus had with the trio at their home brought some unwanted attention from His antagonists. Once they learned that Jesus was there, some came to see Him, as well as take a peek at Lazarus, whom Jesus had raised from the dead. The chief priests, however, wanted Lazarus killed because his life was now drawing people to Jesus as the Christ. People began to turn away from the teaching of the religious leaders and place their faith in Christ instead.

The fact that people were being drawn to Jesus became even more evident the next day as He made His way to Jerusalem for the Passover celebration. When word got out that Jesus was on His way there, some people took palm branches and went out to meet Him, shouting, *"Hosanna! BLESSED IS HE WHO COMES IN THE NAME OF THE LORD"* (John 12:13).

 Write out Psalm 118:25–26.

Hundreds of years before Jesus came to earth, Old Testament prophets predicted many of the events that occurred in His life. Even the seemingly insignificant fact that Christ rode into Jerusalem on a donkey had been prophesied! God orchestrates even the small details in the carrying out of His plan.

Compare John 12:14–15 with the prediction of the coming Messiah in Zechariah 9:9.

Jesus, finding a young donkey, sat on it; as it is written, "Fear not, daughter of Zion; behold, your King is coming, seated on a donkey's colt."
—John 12:14–15

Rejoice greatly, O daughter of Zion! Shout [in triumph,] O daughter of Jerusalem! Behold, your king is coming to you; He is just and endowed with salvation, Humble, and mounted on a donkey, Even on a colt, the foal of a donkey.
—Zechariah 9:9

Christ lived in constant fulfillment of Old Testament prophecies concerning His arrival. Often the fulfillments were overlooked, not noticed—even by His own disciples—until after His death and resurrection.

John 12:20–36
We have seen that Christ spoke repeatedly about a specific *hour* or *time*. Well, that time had finally arrived.

What important time in Christ's ministry had finally arrived according to the following verse?

And Jesus answered them, saying, "The hour has come for the Son of Man to be glorified."
—John 12:23

This was it. Jesus Christ's time had come. It was finally time for Him to be glorified. Jesus began to speak about His overall purpose for coming to earth—His crucifixion.

Jesus alluded to His future death by using the illustration of a grain of wheat (v. 24). A grain of wheat, green on a stalk, is just that: a grain, one single grain. However, if it falls off and dies and becomes planted, it produces more wheat; it produces more far-reaching results than if it holds on to its original place of security.

Discuss the statement Jesus made in John 12:25.

"He who loves his life loses it, and he who hates his life in this world will keep it to life eternal."
—John 12:25

Unlike a grain of wheat, we actually have to make a choice: We can cling determinedly to our stalks of security and perish with them when they meet their eventual ruin. Or we can die to ourselves, trusting the Lord and giving our lives to Him. Then through our offering of selves as living sacrifices (Romans 12:1), He can use our lives in ways beyond our imaginations.

Why do you think it is often easier to hang on to earthly "security stalks" rather than to let go and allow Christ to use our lives?

For us to truly serve Christ, we must follow Him. Following Him means that we must be willing to let go of personal control of our lives and walk where He leads. This entails having the willingness to pack up and move forward physically, spiritually, and emotionally.

When you consider the physical, spiritual, and emotional areas of your life, in which of those three categories do you find it the hardest to follow Christ? Give a brief explanation.

Although each of these areas carries its own set of struggles and demands of faith, we are commanded to trust Christ and go where He leads. We are promised that if we serve Christ, God the Father will honor us (John 12:26).Christ desires our genuine obedience. In return, He promises that the Father will notice and honor our sacrifice.

Christ has gone before us to demonstrate total obedience to His Father. Upon acknowledging what the near future held, Christ admitted to being troubled in His soul. He knew the future. He was neither unaware of nor fully reconciled to the reality of a wooden cross and sharpened nails that awaited Him. Yet He counted the cost and walked forward.

 Despite Jesus Christ's full awareness and even troubled spirit over His impending future, what was His attitude regarding obedience to God the Father?

"Now My soul has become troubled; and what shall I say, 'Father, save Me from this hour'? But for this purpose I came to this hour. Father, glorify Your name." Then a voice came out of heaven: "I have both glorified it, and will glorify it again."
—John 12:27–28

Jesus's ultimate purpose was to glorify His Father. God the Father, being so well pleased in His Son, made His Son the center of salvation and life. Jesus, the Son, was given the promise that when He was lifted up, He would draw all men to Himself. It is through His sacrifice that we are saved, it is His glory that draws people to Him, and it is His power that sustains us. Christ was and still is the core focus of salvation and perseverance in the Christian life.

John 12:37–50

Despite the miracles Christ had performed in the presence of many witnesses, many people still did not believe in Him. They had seen the events with their own eyes, yet they were blind to the spiritual truth of Jesus Christ's identity. We see that even the people's actions toward and disbelief of Jesus were the fulfillment of an Old Testament prophecy.

Compare the following two verses:

"He has blinded their eyes and He hardened their heart, so that they would not see with their eyes and perceive with their heart, and be converted and I heal them."
—John 12:40

"Render the hearts of this people insensitive, their ears dull, and their eyes dim, otherwise they might see with their eyes, hear with their ears, understand with their hearts, and return and be healed."
—Isaiah 6:10

Even among those who did believe, most remained silent. They did not outwardly confess Christ for fear of being discovered and banned from worship in the synagogue:

"Nevertheless many even of the rulers believed in Him, but because of the Pharisees they were not confessing Him, for fear that they would be put out of the synagogue; for they loved the approval of men rather than the approval of God."
—John 12:42–43

In what ways does our silence speak louder about our true convictions than do our words?

Silence often leaves us in a comfortable position of noncommitment. We can be in the center of a heated debate or casual discussion and sit silently, not placing ourselves at odds with any position. Although this may be an appealing option, simply refusing to admit our beliefs on an issue can be one way of denying our faith. We do not have to be expert theologians, but we must be willing to step out and be counted. Yet our motives are far more important than our words or lack of them.

The words of Christ will be our ultimate judge, not the world. We can choose to deny or dismiss His words, but they will be the standard to which we are ultimately held.

What does Christ say about the words He has spoken?

"For I did not speak on My own initiative, but the Father Himself who sent Me has given Me a commandment as to what to say and what to speak. I know that His commandment is eternal life; therefore the things I speak, I speak just as the Father has told Me."
—John 12:49–50

The words of Christ are words that come directly from God the Father, much as we understand the entire Bible, the Scriptures, to be the inspired Word of God to us. To know the Scriptures is to know the heart of God. One cannot know God without an accurate understanding of His Word. It is through Christ and the Scriptures that God has made Himself known to us. When we turn from these two sources, we are turning from God.

In order to fully know and experience life, we must know our Creator. Access to Him is found only through a personal relationship with God the Son, Jesus Christ. We must be willing to die to ourselves and embrace His truth, teachings, and leadership in our lives. What seems irrational to the world is the sanest thing one can do to find true peace and fulfillment. The first step begins by loosening our grips on our "security stalks," whatever they may be, and trusting that when we fall and die to ourselves, Christ will be there to turn that death into abundant life (John 10:10; 12:24).

Personal Reflection

1. Can I honestly say that I would be willing to worship at the feet of Christ in a completely unashamed and vulnerable way as was displayed by Mary in this chapter?

2. If not, what motives are keeping me from doing so? Are my eyes or ears hardened in any way toward the teachings of Christ?

The Word in the World

My Neighbor, Laura: She Was Always Alone

When I first moved into a new apartment, Laura met me on the staircase with a disapproving glance toward my radio. Her first words to me explained her glance: "I have really enjoyed the quietness around here."

That evening, I baked cookies and left them, with a note introducing myself, at the doorstep of all my new neighbors. Since then, Laura has been much friendlier to me.

The Lord has kept Laura before my eyes and on my heart. Pulling into our parking lot on a typical day, I might see Laura jogging around the neighborhood. She was always alone. One day as I pulled into the lot and, as usual, rushed out of my car toward my apartment with the multitude of things on my to-do list swirling around in my head, I sensed God simply saying, "Go talk to Laura." Within a moment, I heard her call my name. She was walking behind me. As we talked, I realized that she lived alone and figuratively carried the weight of the world on her shoulders. She shared some of her fears about being able to financially survive. I asked her if she went to church anywhere, to which she replied no. I shared with her about my church and invited her to attend with me sometime. This allowed us to discuss the roles the church and Christ Jesus have in my life.

Week 13   John 13

Betrayal Is Predicted

> *When Jesus had said this, He became troubled in spirit, and testified and said, "Truly, truly, I say to you, that one of you will betray Me."*
> —John 13:21

John 13:1–11

The hour was quickly approaching—the hour that Jesus Christ had come to earth to face. He lived life to the fullest as our teacher and example. His impending death would provide our victory over sin. Two betrayals were predicted in this chapter: one follower would betray Jesus Christ by handing Him over to officials to be killed, whereas another would deny association with His name. Although Jesus knew all along that some of those closest to Him would betray Him, He loved and taught the disciples equally.

 Have you ever been in a situation in which you were challenged to love and serve someone who had betrayed you? Please explain in light detail.

Thankfully, Christ's love is persistent, despite our actions. I am repeatedly challenged by the magnitude of Christ's love for His followers: *"Having loved His own who were in the world, He loved them to the end"* (John 13:1). Christ's purpose was to love and provide a way of escape from sin for all those who placed their faith in Him. Though the courage and convictions of even His closest comrades wavered, Christ's love endured to the end. This promise of persistent love is ours today. As children of God, having come to Him through faith in His Son, we are lavished with an eternal love from which we can never escape.

 Read aloud Romans 8:35–39. Describe how this concept of eternal affection molds your understanding of the magnitude of Christ's love for you.

Who will separate us from the love of Christ? Will tribulation, or distress, or persecution, or famine, or nakedness, or peril, or sword? Just as it is written, "FOR YOUR SAKE WE ARE BEING PUT TO DEATH ALL DAY LONG; WE WERE CONSIDERED AS SHEEP TO BE SLAUGHTERED." But in all these things we overwhelmingly conquer through Him who loved us. For I am convinced that neither death, nor life, nor angels, nor principalities, nor things present, nor things to come, nor powers, nor height, nor depth, nor any other created thing, will be able to separate us from the love of God, which is in Christ Jesus our Lord.
—Romans 8:35–39

Even before the Passover celebration, Christ knew that Satan had already prepared Judas to betray Him. Rather than running from this betrayer, Christ walked straight toward Him, robed in a servant's cloth, and began to wash his feet. Neither avoidance nor revenge was in His thoughts. He knew this was all part of His Father's plan and submitted to it.

The washing of someone's feet is an important illustration. This was—and still is, I might add—considered to be a lowly job. The disciples had most likely traveled many miles in smelly leather sandals. Dirt was probably caked on their tired, weathered feet, which bore the scars of daily travel by foot. None of the disciples were prepared for their Lord to kneel before them and begin to wash and dry their feet.

 Read the following passage, and describe Peter's first, second, and third responses to Christ's attempt to wash his feet.

So He came to Simon Peter. He said to Him, "Lord, do You wash my feet?" Jesus answered and said to him, "What I do you do not realize now, but you will understand hereafter." Peter said to Him, "Never shall You wash my feet!" Jesus answered him, "If I do not wash you, you have no part with Me." Simon Peter said to Him, "Lord, then wash not only my feet, but also my hands and my head." Jesus said to him, "He who has bathed needs only to wash his feet, but is completely clean; and you are clean, but not all of you."
—John 13:6–10

At first, even Peter could not understand why Jesus Christ was humbling Himself in such a way. Christ explained to Peter that we must first allow Him to serve us in order for us to truly have a part with Him. Christ's servanthood is reflected in the image of Christ kneeling before His disciples to wash their feet, but it is reflected in even greater measure in the later image of Him hanging on the Cross. Jesus did not merely speak about serving and giving His life away—He did it! He knelt, washed feet, and eventually allowed Himself to be pierced for our transgressions. To follow His example, we too must be willing to step down, grab a servant's "towel," and go to serving.

John 13:12–20

Christ did not want His disciples to miss the point of His illustration. Scripture records the fact that once He finished washing their feet, Christ reclined again and basically said, "Hey guys, do you understand what I have just done?" (v. 12). Since He took the time to ensure that they understood, we would be wise to look deeper at this event!

"You call Me Teacher and Lord; and you are right, for so I am. If I then, the Lord and the Teacher, washed your feet, you also ought to wash one another's feet. For I gave you an example that you also should do as I did to you. Truly, truly, I say to you, a slave is not greater than his master, nor is one who is sent greater than the

one who sent him. If you know these things, you are blessed if you
do them."
—John 13:13–17

 According to the preceding passage, what challenge did Christ give the disciples? What is a modern application of this challenge in your own life?

Knowing the Scriptures and applying their truth to our lives have their own rewards. If we practice the things we have been taught to do, we will be blessed (v. 17). True happiness occurs in the process of obedience to God's commands.

During the continuation of this speech that Christ Jesus gave to His disciples, He referred again to the upcoming betrayal (v. 18). What amazes me is that He once again used a prophecy from the Old Testament to point to the present!

 Read Psalm 41:9 and write out the verse.

The time had come for Judas to betray Christ. Judas fulfilled the Psalm 41:9 prophecy as the friend who had eaten with Christ (or shared in a very personal manner). Jesus Christ purposefully brought up this Old Testament prophecy in the Book of Psalms so that the disciples would later recognize the event being fulfilled when it happened.

John 13:21–30

I wish I could have seen the look on the disciples' faces when Christ told them outright, *"One of you will betray Me"* (John 13:21). When I am placed in the awkward position of knowing that someone near me has just been called out and convicted of wrongdoing, I too share that person's embarrassment. Even if I had absolutely nothing to do with the situation, at times I feel just as guilty! We are not given all the details of the disciples' reactions, but we are told that they immediately began to look around at one another. We can definitely assume they were wondering, *Who is He talking about?* Peter finally stepped up to the plate and broached the question everyone else wanted to ask. However, he did not actually ask it himself. Instead, Peter noticed John sitting near Christ and motioned for him to ask.

> *The disciples began looking at one another, at a loss to know of which one He was speaking. There was reclining on Jesus' bosom one of His disciples, whom Jesus loved. So Simon Peter gestured to him, and said to him, "Tell us who it is of whom He is speaking." He, leaning back thus on Jesus' bosom, said to Him, "Lord, who is it?" Jesus then answered, "That is the one for whom I shall dip the morsel and give it to him." So when He had dipped the morsel, He took and gave it to Judas, the son of Simon Iscariot.*
> —John 13:22–26

 What was Jesus's response to the question Peter initiated, and how does His response relate to Psalm 41:9?

Referring to the Old Testament prophecy, Christ Jesus told His disciples exactly who the betrayer would be; yet they still did not understand. Christ dipped the bread and handed it to Judas. Although we are told the others did not understand, we are not given insight into Judas's thoughts. Perhaps he realized what he was about to do; perhaps he did not. Either way, Christ told him, *"What you do, do quickly"* (John 13:27). So Judas left immediately and set out to fulfill the prophecy.

John 13:31–38
When Judas left to fulfill his role in prophecy, the countdown of Jesus's final moments on earth began. Knowing that His time was growing short, Jesus Christ gave His disciples some final words of wisdom.

 Read the following passage, then write the new commandment Jesus Christ gave to His disciples.

> *"Little children, I am with you a little while longer. You will seek Me; and as I said to the Jews, now I also say to you, 'Where I am going,*

you cannot come.' A new commandment I give to you, that you love one another, even as I have loved you, that you also love one another. By this all men will know that you are My disciples, if you have love for one another."
—John 13:33–35

Let us recall what we learned at the beginning of this chapter: Christ loved His followers until the end. That enduring, perfect, unifying love is now a commandment for all believers to possess and exhibit. In times in which it seems normal to throw away relationships with people who do not meet our every desire or fit in our plans, Christ still tells us through the Word that we are to love one another as He loved—to the end. Through living this example of love daily, people will know we are His.

Peter, evidently caught up in Jesus's announcement of His departure, stepped out and asked what they all wanted to know: *"Lord, where are You going?"* (John 13:36). He was probably thinking, *Hey, we have followed you this far. Where are you going now that we cannot go?*

 What was Christ's response (v. 36b) to Peter's question?

We now come to the dramatic moment when Peter proclaimed his total commitment to Jesus: *"Lord, why can I not follow You right now? I will lay down my life for You"* (John 13:37). Can you relate to this moment? Has there ever been a time in your own life when you felt so dedicated and close to the Lord that you made some similar bold statement of commitment, such as, "Lord, I'll do anything for you!" I'm sure Peter, at the time, meant what he said. But Christ knows the future and, therefore, knew that the very same man proclaiming commitment till death was soon to deny he even knew Him.

 Write out Christ's response (v. 38) to Peter's proclamation.

With this response, the stage was set. Judas had been released to begin fulfilling his part of the prophecy, and Peter had been warned that he too would betray his confession of unwavering commitment. These two men were soon to carry out two separate, yet both important, predicted betrayals. Neither betrayal caught Christ off guard. He knew the betrayals were coming, and He allowed both to work toward the completion of God's perfect plan.

Personal Reflection

1. **Having read the scriptural account of Jesus washing the feet of His disciples, do I feel challenged in the way that I should be acting toward fellow believers in my life? What changes are needed?**

2. **If anyone were to examine my life, would that person conclude that I love others? In what areas of my life do I need to concentrate more on learning to love like Christ called me to love?**

The Word in the World

Ana: Testify Boldly That Jesus Is the Way

Ana is one of my hairdressers. She is a Christian and has been sharing about Jesus with her best friend. She took a class on evangelism at her local church and was telling her friend, Karol, about her experience.

Karol, who is not a believer, said, "Ana, I am surprised you are taking the class. You are pretty bold with your faith already."

Ana said, "Not really. You are my best friend, and I have never told you that you are going to hell if you don't accept Jesus Christ as your Savior!"

Now that was bold! The two are still talking. Time will tell what God will do through this.

I Am the Way, the Truth, and the Life

People Introduced
No new people introduced

> *Jesus said to him, "I am the way, and the truth, and the life; no one comes to the Father but through Me."*
> —John 14:6

John 14:1–6

Christ's announcement that He was about to go away and that His disciples could not go with Him right then (John 13:33, 36) was of obvious concern to them. The disciples had just spent approximately three years of their lives following Jesus around, listening to His teachings, learning from the Master, and wholly devoting their lives to Him, only to be told that He was going away and that they could not follow at this time.

Christ saw and immediately addressed the real need of the moment: His disciples were troubled in their hearts. Can you blame them? However, rather than using emotional phrases or group hugs, Christ spoke strong, solid commands.

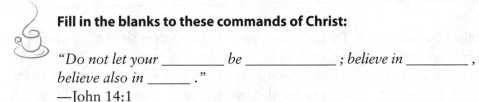

Fill in the blanks to these commands of Christ:

"Do not let your _____ be _____ ; believe in _____ , believe also in _____ ."
—John 14:1

Christ did not deny their feelings; nor did He encourage them to wade around in a pool of emotions. Instead, Christ called them back to faith.

Christ then moved on to tell them where He was going. He spoke about His Father's house, which has historically been interpreted to mean "heaven." Christ told the disciples that He was going away to prepare a place for them in His Father's house, so their separation from Him would not be permanent.

According to John 14:3, what promises are the disciples (and us!) given by Christ?

Note this: Christ—having just told His disciples that He was going somewhere they could not follow at the time—promised that He would return for them (v. 3). Christ did not leave for heaven before letting His followers know that He would come back to get them! Until the moment Christ returns, He is still preparing a place for us. He will return some day for His followers!

Read aloud the following passage from 1 Thessalonians. Discuss the events spoken of in these verses.

For the Lord Himself will descend from heaven with a shout, with the voice of the archangel and with the trumpet of God, and the dead in Christ will rise first. Then we who are alive and remain will be caught up together with them in the clouds to meet the Lord in the air, and so we shall always be with the Lord. Therefore comfort one another with these words.
—1 Thessalonians 4:16–18

We cannot dive into this 1 Thessalonians passage right now, since the purpose of this study is to walk us through the Gospel of John. Yet I could not allow you to read Christ's first promise of His impending return without looking elsewhere in the Scriptures for more information about this event. The promise that our Lord will someday split the sky wide open with a shout and come back for us thrills me beyond words! Hollywood can only dream of such adventure and excitement! Let our hearts not be troubled; let us believe, for we have a King who will return for us.

Pull Up a Chair

How can an understanding of this promise keep our hearts from being troubled by current and future trials and tribulations?

Jesus told His disciples that they *"know the way"* (John 14:4) to His Father's house. The disciples did not immediately understand this statement, for Scripture records Thomas asking, *"How do we know the way?"* (v. 5). I love Thomas, the realist. We will see more of his doubt and confusion in later chapters. But before we convict him of having little faith, let us remember that we have the final answers in our hands (the Scriptures), whereas Thomas and the other disciples did not have the benefit of our New Testament Scriptures as they faith walked these events. If I had been among the disciples on that day, I too might have shared his confusion.

 What important and exclusive role does Christ play in gaining access to God the Father?

Jesus said to him, "I am the way, and the truth, and the life; no one comes to the Father but through Me."
—John 14:6

Christ assured the disciples that because they knew Him, they knew the way to the Father. Jesus Christ alone is the way to God the Father. Christ clearly stated, *"No one comes to the Father but through Me"* (v. 6). Though the world offers many options for getting to heaven, such as morality, sacrifice, and service, Christ clearly tells us that apart from faith in Him, access to heaven is denied.

 Read Acts 4:10–12; then write Acts 4:12 below. How does this verse deny the possibility of obtaining salvation through any faith, practice, or religion other than a relationship with Jesus Christ?

John 14:7–11

We have read repeatedly in the Scriptures that Christ claimed God as His Father. However, in the following passage, a new and important perspective on that relationship is proclaimed.

> *"If you had known Me, you would have known My Father also; from now on you know Him, and have seen Him." Philip said to Him, "Lord, show us the Father, and it is enough for us." Jesus said to him, "Have I been so long with you, and yet you have not come to know Me, Philip? He who has seen Me has seen the Father; how can you say, 'Show us the Father'? Do you not believe that I am in the Father, and the Father is in Me? The words that I say to you I do not speak on My own initiative, but the Father abiding in Me does His works."*
> —John 14:7–10

We are not the only ones to do a double take at this. The disciples had traveled with Christ for years and still Philip asked, *"Lord, show us the Father"* (v. 8), not yet realizing that seeing Christ was equivalent to seeing the Father.

 Explain in your own words the relationship between Jesus Christ and God as stated in John 14:7–10.

In continued response to Philip's question, Christ said, *"Believe Me that I am in the Father and the Father is in Me"* (John 14:11). Jesus Christ was not *partially* God; He was *fully* divine in His makeup (as well as being fully human). The Son of God, who is cocreator of this universe (John 1:3; Hebrews 1:2), left His Father's glory (John 17:5) and came to earth as Jesus, yet remained one with His Father in the aspect of sharing the divine nature (John 10:30).

In John 14, we get a good a glimpse of the mystery of the Trinity—God the Father, God the Son, and God the Holy Spirit. Several seminary professors have explained this mystery of the Trinity to me by using this phrase: "One Essence in three Persons." God the Father, God the Son (Jesus Christ), and the Holy Spirit are three distinct Persons, each of whom are fully God. Thus, all three Persons of the Trinity have existed eternally as one God.

 How is the eternal existence of Christ as part of the Trinity expressed in the following passage from John 1?

In the beginning was the Word, and the Word was with God, and the Word was God. He was in the beginning with God. All things came into being through Him, and apart from Him nothing came into being that has come into being.
—John 1:1–3

John 14:12–14

Next, John records Jesus's explanation of the promise and power of prayer.

"Truly, truly, I say to you, he who believes in Me, the works that I do, he will do also; and greater works than these he will do; because I go to the Father. Whatever you ask in My name, that will I do, so that the Father may be glorified in the Son."
—John 14:12–13

We who believe in Jesus Christ are promised that whatever we ask in Jesus's name, He will do. Be sure to note the purpose of this promise: *"so that the Father may be glorified in the Son"* (v. 13). Our answered prayers are for the purpose of bringing glory to God. So as we pray in the name of Jesus Christ (or His best interests), we can trust that through His answers to our prayers, He is bringing due glory to the Father.

John 14:15–31

A third member of the Trinity, the Holy Spirit (also called Helper, Spirit of truth, Comforter, and Counselor), is spoken of in the passages that follow:

"If you love Me, you will keep My commandments. And I will ask the Father, and He will give you another Counselor to be with you forever. He is the Spirit of truth, whom the world is unable to receive

because it doesn't see Him or know Him. But you do know Him, because He remains with you and will be in you."
—John 14:15–17 (HCSB)

"I have spoken these things to you while I remain with you. But the Counselor, the Holy Spirit, whom the Father will send in My name, will teach you all things and remind you of everything I have told you."
—John 14:25–26 (HCSB)

List everything you learn about the Holy Spirit, the Counselor, from John 14:15–17, 25–26.

Because we, as believers, are indwelt with the Holy Spirit (the Counselor) upon our profession of faith in Christ, we are promised that we will "see" Christ, even though He has currently departed this earth. Through this mighty Counselor, we will be given knowledge and understanding of how to best follow Christ. And following Christ begins with obeying His words.

"He who has My commandments and keeps them is the one who loves Me; and he who loves Me will be loved by My Father, and I will love him and will disclose Myself to him."
—John 14:21

Describe the relationship between our obedience to Christ's words and our love of Jesus Christ (v. 21).

Describe the results we can expect from showing our love for Christ through obedience (v. 21)

As we show our love for Jesus Christ through obedience to His commands, we enter into a holy circle of love, and Christ reveals Himself to us.

Walking daily in relationship with Christ may not always take us down easy paths, but we do have a guarantee of peace.

> *"Peace I leave with you; My peace I give to you; not as the world gives do I give to you. Do not let your heart be troubled, nor let it be fearful."*
> —John 14:27

Because we still walk around in a world that is affected by sin, we will face hardships and troubles. Yet even in the midst of difficult times, we can count on having peace that this world cannot offer—peace that comes only from God.

I cannot leave this chapter without discussing verse 30. Christ made sure that His disciples were aware that Satan is present in this world and that he is real. Satan is referred to as *"the ruler of the world"* (v. 30). In other words, for a time specified by God, Satan has been given derivative or secondary authority to rule and act in various ways on this earth. However, we can find extreme peace in one ultimate truth. And what is that truth?

> *"I will not talk with you much longer, because the ruler of the world is coming. He has no power over Me."*
> —John 14:30 (HCSB)

 According to John 14:30, what is the relationship between Satan's authority and Christ's?

Though Satan (the devil) has power, it is void when it comes against Christ! Satan's power ceases at the foot of Christ. One word from Christ's mouth and Satan is powerless! The One whom we serve ultimately has control over all powers of the earth, including Satan. *"Do not let your heart be troubled, nor let it be fearful"* (John 14:27). We correctly claim our peace when we fully understand and know the true Peace Giver.

Personal Reflection

1. Have I fully grasped the truth that Christ alone is the single path toward a relationship with God?

2. If I have a relationship with Christ, do I live like I understand and believe that He is more powerful than Satan? In what areas of life do I live in unnecessary fear?

The Word in the World

Misty: This Is Out of Her Hands—But in Whose?

Misty is a co-worker who is currently involved in a homosexual lifestyle. Although she has always known that I am a Christian, we had never discussed faith much until several weeks ago.

I began to notice Misty walking around with tears in her eyes. At first she was very unapproachable. She even directly refused to talk with me. However, a few days later, as I knelt beside her desk, I asked how she was doing.

She shared that she had just ended a relationship with her girlfriend and that she felt as though the world was ending. She made an interesting statement: "Everything happens for a purpose, and this is out of my hands."

After listening to this statement, I asked her if she really believed what she had said. If so, into whose hands had she placed it? She looked a little perplexed. I began to share with her the assurance we have that God does indeed have a plan for our lives, yet that plan begins with a personal relationship with Him.

Week 15   John 15

Abide in Me

"I am the vine, you are the branches; he who abides in Me and I in him, he bears much fruit, for apart from Me you can do nothing."
—John 15:5

John 15:1–8

This chapter is an entire monologue by Jesus Christ. He had told His disciples that He was about to leave them, He had made it clear that He would someday return, and then He seized the moment to share how His disciples could maintain a relationship with Him, though everything they knew about walking with Him would be different in just a matter of days. The difference the disciples would encounter—walking in faith, without the benefit of Jesus's physical presence—is our current reality. Though we have never physically seen Christ, we can learn from His teachings in this chapter how to remain close to Him, how to abide in Him.

 In your Bible, underline every occurrence of the phrase *abide in Me* found in John 15:4–7. (If you don't want to write in your Bible, circle the phrases in the text below.)

"Abide in Me, and I in you. As the branch cannot bear fruit of itself unless it abides in the vine, so neither can you unless you abide in Me. I am the vine, you are the branches; he who abides in Me and I in him, he bears much fruit, for apart from Me you can do nothing. If anyone does not abide in Me, he is thrown away as a branch and

dries up; and they gather them, and cast them into the fire and they are burned. If you abide in Me, and My words abide in you, ask whatever you wish, and it will be done for you."
—John 15:4–7

I was struck by the frequency that Christ used the phrase *abide in Me* when speaking with His disciples. He could have given them a litany of tasks to do in His absence; instead, He repeatedly instructed them to abide in Him. Christ is far less interested in what we are doing *for Him* than in whether we are remaining *in Him*. What a relief! We do not have to perform for Christ. We must merely stay in His presence and allow Him to do the guiding.

So how do we abide in Him? Jesus answered this question by using the illustration of a vine and its branches. The vine is the total source of nutrition and sustenance for the branches. If they somehow break away from that source, they will surely die. As the branches must stay attached to the vine to survive, so we too must stay connected to Christ, daily drawing our nutrients from Him to sustain our lives.

 List and discuss several ways that we abide in Christ (for example, Bible study).

Our abiding in Christ glorifies God. Just as a healthy vine produces good fruit according to its kind, our lives, when connected to Christ, produce good spiritual fruit.

 Read the following passage out loud, and circle the individual fruits of the Spirit that develop in us as we abide in Christ.

But the fruit of the Spirit is love, joy, peace, patience, kindness, goodness, faithfulness, gentleness, self-control; against such things there is no law.
—Galatians 5:22–23

These characteristics in our lives are evidence that we are abiding in Christ. Through a continual, daily walk with Christ, we are given the opportunity to grow and sharpen these virtues. Though our natural inclinations lean toward selfishness and pride, growth in Christ lessens evidence of those undesirable inclinations and produces good fruit that is evident to all.

John 15:9–17

In this section of John 15, Christ spoke specifically about love—not the fleeting emotive type, but enduring, eternal love. Christ compared His love toward His followers with nothing less than the love of His Father toward Him.

 Write John 15:9 below.

The love that we are commanded to abide in is perfect, holy, and eternal. It is, in essence, the same love that is forever being passed between God the Father and God the Son. We share in this divine love through our faith in Christ.

 Compare John 14:21 with John 15:10. In light of these verses, why is it important for Christians to know Christ's commands?

"He who has My commandments and keeps them is the one who loves Me; and he who loves Me will be loved by My Father, and I will love him and will disclose Myself to him."
—John 14:21

"If you keep My commandments, you will abide in My love; just as I have kept My Father's commandments and abide in His love."
—John 15:10

In order for us to fully grow as believers, it is essential for us to know Christ's commands. These are found through the study of God's Word. Knowledge of the Scriptures enables us to be obedient to Christ and indwelt with His abiding love and joy.

Fill in the blanks to complete the following verse:

"These things I have _____ to you so that _____ _____ may be in you, and that _____ _____ may be made full."
—John 15:11

Christ next issued a command to love one another as He had demonstrated love (v. 12). His love eventually took Him to a cruel cross where He willingly laid down His life for the benefit of all people. Although we may not all be called to surrender our physical lives to the point of death, we are all issued the command to deny self (Matthew 16:24), to put away selfishness. A passage in Philippians steers us away from selfishness and guides us to look out for the good of others:

> *Do nothing from selfishness or empty conceit, but with humility of mind regard one another as more important than yourselves; do not merely look out for your own personal interests, but also for the interests of others.*
> —Philippians 2:3–4

We are to think higher of others than of ourselves, and we ought to be as quick to look out for the good of someone else as we are for our own gain. Again, this goes against our human nature. Yet, in Christ, we are indwelt with the power to extend love beyond our normal limitations as we allow Christ to rule in us.

John 15:18–27

The emotive tide turns here ever so swiftly. Christ switched from speaking about love to predicting persecution. Do you recall the brief reference to this in chapter 7 when Jesus spoke to His brothers? Christ spoke candidly about immediate and future persecution in John 15:18–25. He was hated first. Christ walked before us and was nailed to a cross for His confessions. We are still living in the same world that drove nails into our Savior's hands. Why then are we shocked when we are treated unkindly for following His commands?

Can you think of a time when you (or persons you know) were persecuted for following the commands of Christ? If so, describe the situation.

If you can personally recall a moment, I hope that you stood firm in your faith. If you cannot, I pray that when the time does come, you will be found faithful. When we unite ourselves with Christ, we gain eternity but may very well lose some earthly treasures or accolades. Let us throw aside any hindrance that causes us to shy away from hardships caused by faithfulness to Christ, remembering that ours is an eternal inheritance.

 According to John 15:23, what further implication is made against those who hate Christ?

It is impossible to hate Jesus Christ and love God. Think on this for a moment. Should the world try to sell us the lies that Jesus was a false prophet and that anyone can know and love God while choosing to reject Christ, John 15:23 speaks loudly in opposition. To love Christ is to love God. To hate Christ is to hate God.

 Reflecting on the statement, "To love Christ is to love God," write at least two reasons it is important for us to abide in Christ.

Personal Reflection

1. Does the understanding that Christ has already set an example of obedience in the fact that He consistently kept His Father's commands help me develop consistency in my obedience to Him? In what specific areas of my life do I need to develop that consistency?

2. Have I ever felt like the world hated me because of my faith in Christ? If I have never felt distinct from the unbelieving world because of my faith, is it possible that I have watered down my faith in order to blend in with the world? If so, what specific areas of compromise come to mind?

The Word in the World

Katy and Chandler: Young in Christ Need Discipling

Late one night while sitting on my couch with the intention of starting to write another chapter of *Pull Up a Chair*, I heard a knock at my door. It was Katy, my 14-year-old neighbor, asking to borrow some CDs. Through this encounter, I discovered that she is a Christian. However, due to frequent moves (her mom being single), Katy had received little, if any, discipleship. She noticed the study on my couch and asked if she and I could begin working through it. That very night, we went to a photocopy shop—pajamas and all—and made a copy of the study for her.

Our first planned meeting was at a well-frequented bookstore. When we first got there, Katy asked if she could look around for a moment. She noticed a friend in the music section. She then walked straight up to her friend Chandler and invited her to come join us.

Chandler replied, "Why are you studying the Bible?"

Katy answered, "So I can learn more about God. Duh!"

"Oh," said Chandler. "Well, I'm not, like, Jewish or anything; I'm OK with studying the Bible." They both joined me that night.

We met the next week at my home. Katy reminded me that the study had been tentatively titled *Java and John*, and that sharing it over coffee was really a good idea. So off we went to a local coffee shop.

Week 16　　John 16

Look: An Hour Is Coming

People Introduced
No new people introduced

"Behold, an hour is coming, and has already come, for you to be scattered, each to his own home, and to leave Me alone; and yet I am not alone, because the Father is with Me."
—John 16:32

John 16:1–15
The information keeps coming! Christ was fully aware that His time with the disciples was drawing to an end, and He was very intent on leaving them informed and confident.

Can you imagine what Christ's disciples must have felt like that evening, getting all of this teaching in one major crash course? Even if they felt overwhelmed, Christ had a distinct purpose for providing this wellspring of information.

According to John 16:1, for what purpose were the disciples given all of the information recorded in John 13–15?

I am so thankful that we have Christ's messages written down so we can easily glance back over them and refresh our memories. Knowledge of the Scriptures keeps us from "stumbling" our way through life. God did not intend for us to walk around aimlessly, each of us trying to define ourselves and create paths to Him or to our own happiness. Rather, through Christ and the Scriptures, God has given us knowledge to assist us in our navigation. Without an accurate understanding of His Word, we are sure to trip over many roadblocks along our paths.

As mentioned in John 14, we have another guide to help us journey through life: our Counselor (the Holy Spirit). Christ was so confident in the unique roles of the Counselor that He told the disciples it was for their benefit that He was leaving, because when He went away, the Counselor would come. Through this statement, we can see that the work and the roles of the Counselor were never meant to be considered second-class to those of God the Father or Christ the Son.

According to John 16:8, in what three areas will the Counselor convict the world?

Thankfully, it is the role of the Holy Spirit to convict the world. This is neither our job nor obligation. Actually, we can potentially do damage when we step outside our role of messenger and try to take on the role of a "mini–Holy Spirit" in someone else's life. We are to share the love and truth of Christ with everyone we meet, but the Holy Spirit is the One who is to convict them of sin, righteousness, and judgment.

Describe a situation in which someone may have wrong notions of acting as a mini–Holy Spirit in someone else's life.

The work of the Holy Spirit is vast. He not only is at work in the hearts of nonbelievers but plays an important role in the lives of believers as well.

Read the following verses, and list the promises given to believers regarding the help of the Holy Spirit.

"When they bring you before the synagogues and the rulers and the authorities, do not worry about how or what you are to speak in your

defense, or what you are to say; for the Holy Spirit will teach you in that very hour what you ought to say."
—Luke 12:11–12

"But the Helper, the Holy Spirit, whom the Father will send in My name, He will teach you all things, and bring to your remembrance all that I said to you."
—John 14:26

"But when He, the Spirit of truth, comes, He will guide you into all the truth; for He will not speak on His own initiative, but whatever He hears, He will speak; and He will disclose to you what is to come. He will glorify Me, for He will take of Mine and will disclose it to you."
—John 16:13–14

"But you will receive power when the Holy Spirit has come upon you; and you shall be My witnesses both in Jerusalem, and in all Judea and Samaria, and even to the remotest part of the earth."
—Acts 1:8

Retain the standard of sound words which you have heard from me, in the faith and love which are in Christ Jesus. Guard, through the Holy Spirit who dwells in us, the treasure which has been entrusted to you.
—2 Timothy 1:13–14

John 16:16–24

Do you ever laugh while reading the Scriptures? I do. I am thrilled that God decided to leave in the human moments of our predecessors in the faith. In their occasional confusion, doubt, and fear, I see myself. This makes it easier for me to rejoice with them over their moments of faith and victories.

In John 16:16–18, Christ spoke what seemed to be a riddle; He mentioned that His disciples would not see Him, then they would see Him. I can get lost in the wording in that passage. But, thankfully, I am not alone. This Scripture honestly records the initial confusion of the disciples as well. The disciples even questioned and said to one another, *"What is this that He says...? We do not know what He is talking about"* (John 16:18).

Christ addressed their question even before they asked Him directly (v. 19). What joy it brings to know that Christ is aware of our fears and confusion even before we bring them to Him. He is not only aware but also faithful and ready with answers.

Many biblical scholars believe that the next few verses foreshadow Christ's approaching time on the Cross. Christ warned the disciples that a time of sorrow and weeping was coming; however, during their time of grief, the world would rejoice (v. 20). While Christ hung on the Cross, many in the world and Satan naïvely rejoiced, falsely believing that they had conquered the Man called Christ. Yet, as we will read later, their rejoicing was premature.

 What promises did Christ give concerning His disciples' grief (v. 22)?

"Therefore you too have grief now; but I will see you again, and your heart will rejoice, and no one will take your joy away from you."
—John 16:22

Christ made an important prediction about Himself in this verse (v. 22). He stated that though the disciples would have grief (referring to His upcoming death by crucifixion), He would see them again (referring to His resurrection). Christ was preparing His disciples for His death with a promise of future joy that, when given, could not be stolen by the world. This joy would result from seeing Him alive again.

As modern-day believers, we do not see Christ's death as an end. We know now that Christ arose from the dead three days after His crucifixion. And the joy promised the disciples is available also to those of us today who have placed our faith in Jesus Christ, the *risen* Son of God.

John 16:25–33

Can you imagine the sigh of relief that must have come from the disciples when Christ promised them that a time would come when He would no longer speak in parables or *"figurative language"* (v. 25)? I can just hear one or two saying, "Finally! Maybe then we will understand something the first time around!"

In verse 27, Christ made a precious statement that should have been clear-cut enough for anyone to understand, and it applied not only to the disciples but also to all believers and continues to apply to believers today.

Read John 16:27 and fill in the following blanks:

"For the _____ _____ loves you, because you have _____ _____ and have _____ that I came forth from the Father."
—John 16:27

God the Father lavishes His love on all of us who love Jesus Christ and believe that He came from the Father. In Christ, we are not only sheltered from the wrath of God but also covered in His mercy and love. Although the pronoun *you* in the original Greek text for verse 27 is plural, it is also true that God loves us individually, not merely as a mass unit. God does not look down on us and see a swarming ant bed of human existence. Rather, He loves us as individuals and prepares a specific plan for each of our lives.

Do you live your life more in line with the understanding that God loves you as an individual or that He loves you as a part of a mass society?

I am convinced that our answer to the above question greatly affects how we walk through life. Please take a moment to grasp this truth: God loves *you* as an individual. He wants *you* to know Him and have a personal relationship with Him. Yes, once we are believers, we join an amazing family of faith, yet that membership is acquired through our individual decisions to place our faith in Jesus Christ.

Having joined ourselves to God through faith in Christ does not mean that we will walk through life without troubles or hardships. Actually, it can mean just the opposite. At the end of John 16, we see that Christ warned His disciples that they would have suffering in this world, yet He would be a source of peace and strength to them.

 Write out John 16:33 in the following space.

We are commanded by Christ to *"take courage."* Our courage is not, nor should it be, founded in ourselves; rather, it is to be sourced in Jesus Christ. He let us know that He has *"overcome the world"* (v. 33).

Even though the world seems crazy and out of control at times, Ephesians 1, Isaiah 46:10, and other passages in the Scriptures indicate to us that God has everything under control. This same God who directs every affair of nature and mankind is the same One who loves us abundantly when our faith is in God the Son, Jesus Christ.

Personal Reflection

1. How does the understanding that God promises to give me wisdom in His perfect timing regarding any situation in my life cause me to further trust Him?

2. In what ways do I lean on the wisdom of the Holy Spirit? What practices or disciplines are present in my life that help me to hear and obey God?

The
Word
in the World

Mrs. C: Does Praying Hands Pendant Reflect Lifestyle?

Mrs. C was 68 years old and recently diagnosed with breast cancer when I met her. I stepped into the room to draw her blood and was immediately told, "I hope you know what you are doing; I don't want to be your guinea pig."

I smiled and said, "Guinea pigs are out. We use white mice now."

"Fine then. I don't want to be your white mouse!" she replied.

Next, she asked to see my name badge. I had to confess that I had left it at home on my dresser. Hearing this, she questioned whether I was really a nurse. Once she was sufficiently satisfied with my credentials, I drew blood for her blood work.

A stream of blood went down her arm, and she exclaimed, "Good grief! You are making a mess!"

Experiencing a temporary loss of patience, I exclaimed, "My goodness, you are grumpy, aren't you?"

A snicker escaped her, softening her seasoned face, which was now framed by her newly acquired baldness. Our relationship began there. I noticed she was wearing a Praying Hands pendant, so I asked her if she prayed. She said that she did sometimes, but she denied going to church anywhere. She said that she lived alone and then began sharing about the struggles that come along with aging, illness, and isolation. I shared with her the love of Christ and how she could have a relationship with Him. She did not make a decision that day, but she remains in my prayers.

Pull Up a Chair

Week 17   John 17

Jesus Prays

Future believers, including us (those who believe in Christ through the words of the disciples)

> *"I do not ask on behalf of these alone, but for those also who believe in Me through their word; that they may all be one; even as You, Father, are in Me and I in You, that they also may be in Us, so that the world may believe that You sent Me."*
> —John 17:20–21

If I could be a figurative fly on the wall during any time in history, I would choose the time when Jesus Christ, after having shared His final meal and a time of instruction with His disciples, prayed to His Father. Envision with me a moment that is uniquely mixed with both serenity and honest anguish. The *hour* or *moment* Christ had been referring to was bearing down on Him. This moment was not coming as a surprise, for we have seen that He had repeatedly spoken of its arrival; yet when it came, it was laced with human dread of pain, solitude, and abandonment. This hour was one through which Christ must suffer alone. No friend could go with Him or take His place.

Although exact details of Christ's physical surroundings during this time are left to our imaginations, the Scriptures do give us a careful record of His prayer. When faced with certain difficulty, Christ's first reaction was to go to His Father. He did not sit around the campfire, questioning His disciples about what He should do next. Instead, He prostrated Himself before God the Father.

When faced with a difficult situation, what is your first reaction?
- ❑ **Ask the advice of friends.**
- ❑ **Go to God in prayer.**
- ❑ **Study the examples of others in similar situations.**
- ❑ **Other** _____

Christ is our example of how we should respond in times of difficulty. Although studying examples of others is wise and asking the advice of trusted friends is often helpful, seeking God about the matter should be our primary response. He preeminently has the answers to every situation we face.

John 17:1–5

As we look carefully at Jesus Christ's prayer to His Father, we see it can be divided into three sections: a prayer for Himself, a prayer for His disciples, and a prayer for all believers. Let us look first at His prayer for Himself.

According to John 17:1, what was the overriding purpose of Jesus's impending hour of trial?

Bringing glory to God was Christ's primary purpose. Despite the pain or suffering He would have to endure, His main intention was to honor and glorify His Father. This is a convicting reminder of how we, as believers, ought to face trials. Though we do not need to deny the hardships we may endure, our focus ought to be more on how each event will bring glory to God rather than what we might face or ultimately lose.

Read the following passage aloud. What is Jesus's own definition of eternal life?

Jesus spoke these things; and lifting up His eyes to heaven, He said, "Father, the hour has come; glorify Your Son, that the Son may glorify You, even as You gave Him authority over all flesh, that to all

whom You have given Him, He may give eternal life. This is eternal life, that they may know You, the only true God, and Jesus Christ whom You have sent."
—John 17:1–3

Salvation is not accidentally discovered. According to the Scriptures, a person does not happen upon a relationship with God without first meeting one specific requirement. In the preceding passage, Jesus prayed that He would correctly fulfill the demand of salvation—that is, reveal God the Father and Himself as God the Son to all those whom the Father gave Him. A lack of knowing either—the Father or the Son—would nullify a person's positive involvement in God's biblical plan of salvation.

Christ ended the first part of His prayer with a request to be glorified in a way that He previously experienced *"before the world was"* (v. 5). Once again, we see how Scriptures constantly build upon truth throughout the pages of God's Word.

 Discuss the significance of John 1:1 as you compare it with John 17:5.

In the beginning was the Word, and the Word was with God, and the Word was God.
—John 1:1

"Now, Father, glorify Me together with Yourself, with the glory which I had with You before the world was."
—John 17:5

John 17:6–19

At this point, the focus of Christ's prayer shifted from Himself to His disciples. He declared that He had been faithful to reveal God's name and purpose to them, and that they had been faithful in keeping His word (v. 6). Of all the things Jesus Christ could have said about the disciples, notice that the initial thought was that these guys had stuck by the truth Jesus had taught them.

At this point in your life, would Christ be able to say the following about you?

"Thank you, Father, for _____ (write your name). She has been faithful in keeping my Word."

Thinking over my life, I realize my answer would vary depending on what season of my life I was in when I answered the question. Thankfully, we are encouraged to press on toward the goal of obedience, recognizing that obedience is valued above performing good deeds or having good behavior. If we can focus on being obedient children of God, the other virtues will naturally follow. I am so thankful for this. If I had to refine godly virtues in my life on my own, I would forever be in a cycle of disappointment!

Next, Christ's prayer focused on the protection of His disciples. He specifically said, *"I do not ask on behalf of the world, but of those whom You have given Me"* (John 17:9), illustrating the personal nature of His prayer. He knew that the disciples were about to face difficult times. His prayer dealt with the reality of the situation and sought help and guidance from God.

 According to the following passage, whose name was the source of the disciples' protection?

"I am no longer in the world; and yet they themselves are in the world, and I come to You. Holy Father, keep them in Your name, the name which You have given Me, that they may be one even as We are. While I was with them, I was keeping them in Your name which You have given Me."
—John 17:11–12

Twice in these two verses, Jesus Christ referred to the disciples' protection being found in the name of God the Father. He is their source of strength, protection, endurance, and hope not only for eternal salvation but for life on earth as well. I love the way the psalmist who wrote Psalm 20 expressed his understanding of this truth.

Read Psalm 20:7, and fill in the following blanks with your own personal choices:

Some boast in _____ and some in _____ , but we will boast in the name of the LORD, our God.
—Personal paraphrase of Psalm 20:7

Jesus, with the realization that He would soon be departing this world, prayed that the disciples might have His joy made full in them through the words He had spoken to them (John 17:13). The words that would bring them joy are in the very Word we have today. The Scriptures are the perfect, holy, and timeless Word of God. When we study and know His truths, we have the opportunity to experience joy that this world cannot take away, though it tries! Jesus knew the world tries to steal joy. Therefore, He prayed that God the Father would protect the disciples from a world that would hate them (vv. 14–15).

As believers, our true citizenship changes from being merely an identity on a passport. Far beyond our call of national duty, we are called to serve and obey our heavenly Father. This service will sometimes contradict society norms and may possibly place us at odds with others over situations that compromise God's truth. Therefore, it is imperative that we understand God's truth.

Write John 17:17.

Christ's final prayer for His disciples was that they know truth—that they be cleansed and kept clean by the truth. Unlike modern society's cry for each of us to define truth for ourselves, truth has not been left up to the opinions of individuals. Christ, speaking to His Father, said, *"Your word is truth"* (v. 17). Not just any fleeting trend or opinion will sanctify and keep us. We must define our ideas about truth based on the standard of God's Word—not vice versa.

John 17:20–26
This section of Christ's prayer is where we come into the picture! Can you believe it? Close to two thousand years ago, before you were even a glimmer in your earthly father's eye, Christ was already praying for future believers, including *you* if you

are a believer in Christ! Jesus Christ already knew your face and your name. The same goes for me. He brought today's believers into the picture when He said, *"I do not ask on behalf of these alone [the disciples], but for those also who believe in Me through their word"* (John 17:20). The word *those* in that passage refers to all Christians! Any one who has come to faith in Christ since the time of the disciples has done so as a result of the disciples' word.

So what was Christ praying about on our behalf? Basically it comes down to one word: *unity.*

 Read aloud John 17:21–23. Underline both occurrences of the phrase *be one* and all other phrases related to unity.

"That they may all be one; even as You, Father, are in Me and I in You, that they also may be in Us, so that the world may believe that You sent Me. The glory which You have given Me I have given to them, that they may be one, just as We are one; I in them and You in Me, that they may be perfected in unity, so that the world may know that You sent Me, and loved them, even as You have loved Me."
—John 17:21–23

At the beginning of this passage, Christ expressed His desire that believers be one just as God the Father and He, God the Son, are one (v. 21). That's a huge goal! Think about it. We have already discussed in previous chapters that God the Father and the Son, Jesus Christ, are knitted together in their very essence. We are to be so intimately connected (knitted) to our brothers and sisters in Christ that their needs become as important as our own.

The last part of this passage gives the vital purpose of our unity: to show the image of God's love (v. 23). Through our relationships with one another, we are given the opportunity to express the divine mystery of God—He is love (1 John 4:8).

Christ did not close His prayer without expressing His final desire for us. Christ stated His longing for the day when all those who have placed their faith in Him will join Him in heaven (v. 24).

Although the world does not know God the Father on its own, Christ made His name known. And His name will continually be made known through the working of the Holy Spirit and the Scriptures so that the love that the Father has for the Son may be in us as believers.

Personal Reflection

1. If I have a relationship with Christ, how does it make me feel to realize that Christ was praying for me before my birth?

2. If I do not have a relationship with Christ, why am I resisting coming into a relationship with the One who continually promises to love and protect me?

The Word in the World

Margie: I'm Scared

Margie had been attending our youth group for a few months and was quickly becoming a part of our church family. This blonde 12-year-old immediately stole my heart. Between her constant desire to sit near me when riding in the church van and her vitality in youth meetings, I came to know her well and feel very close to her.

During one Sunday morning service, I sensed the Lord leading me to pray specifically for Margie. I knew that she had not yet placed her faith in Christ, so as the pastor called for a time of decision, I bowed my head and prayed that God would convict Margie of her need for Him and give her the courage to walk forward. After the prayer, I opened my eyes to see Margie still standing where she had been, yet her eyes were damp with tears and her hands were suspiciously gripping very tightly the pew in front of her.

As soon as the service was dismissed, I walked directly to Margie. Looking at her precious face, I said, "Margie, the Lord placed you on my heart today during the service. May I ask what is keeping you from giving your life to Him?"

In a sudden spring of tears, Margie confessed, "I'm scared."

We sat on the front pew in the church, talked through what it means to give one's life to Christ, and addressed the fear she was facing. That same day, I had the honor of praying with Margie as she came to faith in Christ and received Him as Savior.

Within a few months, Margie was baptized. And you can surely guess who was standing beside her holding her towel in the baptismal pool.

Week 18   John 18

Jesus Is Betrayed

People Introduced

This lesson is packed with important people and events leading up to the crucifixion of Christ. Rather than merely listing the new names introduced in this chapter, I have chosen to include some important details about their lives and the roles they played in Jesus's "trial." My hope is that with a little extra information about these people, you will have deeper understanding of what we are about to study.

Annas (sort of a high priest emeritus): The soldiers first brought Jesus to Annas, who sent Jesus, still bound, to Caiaphas, the ruling high priest.

Caiaphas (the ruling high priest): The role of the high priest was almost always a political office. Caiaphas held this position from A.D. 18 to A.D. 36. He is known historically as the one who declared it is better for one man to die for the nation than for the nation as a whole to perish. After Jesus was brought before Caiaphas, the religious leaders took Jesus to Pilate because they wanted Jesus killed and they could not (according to their dictates) put anyone to death.

Pilate (the Roman governor): Some of Jesus's fellow countrymen brought Him before Pilate because, as a Roman governor, Pilate was in a position to pronounce the sentence of death, whereas Jews were not then allowed by their Roman overlords to put anyone to death. Therefore, Pilate was in a perfect position to demand the punishment the religious leaders desired. Pilate struggled with the decision of whether to sentence Jesus to death. Personally, he found no guilt in Jesus. Therefore, in a last-ditch effort, Pilate offered to set one prisoner free, hoping the crowd would choose Jesus, but the crowd chose Barabbas instead of Jesus the Christ. Pilate had Jesus scourged and eventually handed Him over to be crucified.

Barabbas (an incarcerated criminal): He was arrested for robbery and murder. He gained his freedom because the crowd chose him to be released instead of Christ.

Now Judas also, who was betraying Him, knew the place, for Jesus had often met there with His disciples. Judas then, having received the Roman cohort and officers from the chief priests and the Pharisees, came there with lanterns and torches and weapons.
—John 18:2–3

One of the slaves of the high priest, being a relative of the one whose ear Peter cut off, said, "Did I not see you in the garden with Him?" Peter then denied it again, and immediately a rooster crowed.
—John 18:26–27

In John 18, we see the fulfillment of both betrayals Christ predicted in chapter 13. We see the arrival of the *hour* to which He often referred. We may feel a tugging at our hearts as we read about one disciple's emotive reaction in defense of Christ, followed by the same disciple's triple denial of Him. And our anger may be stirred as we see how another disciple's betrayal led to the capture and death of our Lord.

John 18:1–14

When Jesus had finished praying, He went with His disciples to a garden that they all knew well. We can imagine that they had spent many evenings there talking, learning from Christ as He taught them, and sharing life together. This evening, however, the garden would be infiltrated with something other than friendship—it would experience the bitter taste of betrayal.

 Discuss how the events in John 18:2–3 fulfill the prophecy in John 13:21–30.

Now Judas also, who was betraying Him, knew the place, for Jesus had often met there with His disciples. Judas then, having received the Roman cohort and officers from the chief priests and the Pharisees, came there with lanterns and torches and weapons.
—John 18:2–3

When Jesus had said this, He became troubled in spirit, and testified and said, "Truly, truly, I say to you, that one of you will betray Me."
—John 13:21

He [disciple Jesus loved], leaning back thus on Jesus' bosom, said to Him, "Lord, who is it?" Jesus then answered, "That is the one for whom I shall dip the morsel and give it to him." So when He had dipped the morsel, He took and gave it to Judas, the son of Simon Iscariot. After the morsel, Satan then entered into him. Therefore Jesus said to him, "What you do, do quickly."
—John 13:25–27

Loyalty is a characteristic that is precious to me, so I find myself very angry with Judas for betraying Christ. How dare he sell out his Friend! If you share this reaction with me, let me comfort you with this reminder: Christ was not taken by surprise. He knew Judas would betray Him; He allowed the betrayal to take place so that God's plan would proceed to completion. The Scriptures do not lead us to feel sorry for Christ. He does not need our sympathy, nor does He want it. But He does demand our respect and honor.

We see the lack of surprise in Christ through His immediate response to the Roman soldiers. After they twice expressed their intent to find *"Jesus the Nazarene,"* Christ responded both times, *"I am He"* (vv. 5, 8). The disciples were not ever at risk of being harmed. Christ knew the soldiers were coming and went forth, prepared to meet them.

 How was Christ's response in John 18:8 the fulfillment of His prayer for the disciples that we studied in John 17:12?

Jesus answered, "I told you that I am He; so if you seek Me, let these go their way," to fulfill the word which He spoke, "Of those whom You have given Me I lost not one."
—John 18:8–9

"While I was with them, I was keeping them in Your name which You have given Me; and I guarded them and not one of them perished but the son of perdition, so that the Scripture would be fulfilled."
—John 17:12

The safety of Christ's disciples was never in question. This is a wonderful reminder to us that the Lord cannot accidentally lose us! Every aspect of our lives is lived under the watchful eye of our Lord. Even when circumstances look doubtful, He is in control.

 How did Peter's reaction recorded in the following verse demonstrate his understanding of the situation?

> *Simon Peter then, having a sword, drew it and struck the high priest's slave, and cut off his right ear.*
> —John 18:10

I appreciate Peter's heart. There was something valiant in his desire to defend his Friend. However, his response was wrong. Despite my natural inclination to want to applaud his courage, Christ went straight to the heart of the matter by rebuking the action.

 Summarize Christ's main point in His response to Peter's action.

> *So Jesus said to Peter, "Put the sword into the sheath; the cup which the Father has given Me, shall I not drink it?"*
> —John 18:11

Jesus was concerned more about fulfilling His Father's plan than about His own personal safety. God's glory was of greater importance than His physical well-being. Therefore, He allowed Himself to be tied, led to the Temple, and brought before Annas to be judged.

John 18:15–18 and 25–27

The remaining verses in this lesson will be covered in groupings of associated text rather than in exact order. We will first see the fulfillment of the second predicted betrayal and then look closely at Jesus's encounter with the high priest.

According to John 18:15–16, what was Peter doing after Jesus had been arrested?

Simon Peter was following Jesus, and so was another disciple. Now that disciple was known to the high priest, and entered with Jesus into the court of the high priest, but Peter was standing at the door outside. So the other disciple, who was known to the high priest, went out and spoke to the doorkeeper, and brought Peter in.
—John 18:15–16

Peter was slinking around the trial area where the Roman cohort and Jewish officials had taken his Lord. We just witnessed Peter's display of commitment to Christ (v. 10), yet we are about to see that he wavered in his faithfulness.

Then the slave-girl who kept the door said to Peter, "You are not also one of this man's disciples, are you?" He said, "I am not." Now the slaves and the officers were standing there, having made a charcoal fire, for it was cold and they were warming themselves; and Peter was also with them, standing and warming himself.
—John 18:17–18

Now Simon Peter was standing and warming himself. So they said to him, "You are not also one of His disciples, are you?" He denied it, and said, "I am not." One of the slaves of the high priest, being a relative of the one whose ear Peter cut off, said, "Did I not see you in the garden with Him?" Peter then denied it again, and immediately a rooster crowed.
—John 18:25–27

Referring to John 18:17–18, 25–27 above, list in the chart on the next page the three accounts that fulfill Christ's prediction found in John 13:38:

Jesus answered, "Will you lay down your life for Me? Truly, truly, I say to you, a rooster will not crow until you deny Me three times."
—John 13:38

Question 1	Peter's Response
_____	_____
_____	_____
Question 2	**Peter's Response**
_____	_____
_____	_____
Question 3	**Peter's Response**
_____	_____
_____	_____

 What occurred after the third denial?

Wow! What can you say after an event such as this? I cannot begin to imagine what went through Peter's mind when he heard that rooster crow, reminding him of Jesus's words. We are not all given an audible reminder when we do or say something unfaithful to God; however, we are blessed with His Word, which provides the standard to which we are compared, and the Holy Spirit, who teaches that standard and convicts us when we miss it.

 Can you think of a "rooster crow" moment in your life when God, through His Holy Spirit, convicted you of not standing firm in your commitment to Him? If so, please write a brief description.

John 18:19–24 and 28–40

Verse 19 brings us back to the scenario of Christ standing before the high priest. He had been bound, taken before Annas, and questioned. The first and only question

Pull Up a Chair

went something like this: "Tell us about your disciples and your teachings." Jesus responded by stating that He had always spoken openly and in public places where others, especially His fellow countrymen, were able to hear Him.

From your studies, list a few open and public places where Jesus taught.

Jesus then told the high priest to ask those who had heard Him teach; they could share what they had learned from Him. This response was met with a slap from a temple police officer. Apparently, speaking back in any way other than a direct answer was intolerable in this early judicial system.

Upon reading John 18:23–24, why do you believe Annas decided to send Jesus away? Do you believe it demonstrated his inability to find any true fault in Christ? How?

Because Annas was not officially sanctioned by the Romans, he sent Jesus Christ to Caiaphas, the reigning Jewish high priest. John did not record what happened when Jesus was brought before Caiaphas and the Jewish supreme council, but Matthew and Mark stated that Caiaphas accused Jesus of speaking blasphemy and that the other officials condemned Jesus Christ to be deserving of death (Matthew 26:63–66; Mark 10:60–64). Christ was then moved on to Pilate's headquarters. This was beginning to seem like a perpetual game of "hot potato."

After reading about the encounter between Pilate and the Jewish accusers in John 18:29–32, write a one-sentence summary of the religious leaders' main purpose for bringing Christ before Pilate.

Therefore Pilate went out to them and said, "What accusation do you bring against this Man?" They answered and said to him, "If this Man were not an evildoer, we would not have delivered Him to you." So Pilate said to them, "Take Him yourselves, and judge Him according to your law." The Jews said to him, "We are not permitted

to put anyone to death," to fulfill the word of Jesus which He spoke, signifying by what kind of death He was about to die.
—John 18:29–32

Jews, being under Roman rule at that time, were not permitted to put anyone to death, so they could not sentence Jesus to be crucified. However, crucifixion was the most common form of Roman punishment for the worst of criminals. Jesus Christ knew this type of death awaited Him. The Cross of Christ had been planned from eternity past, and the Lord maneuvered even through petty rules and laws of man to see His plan accomplished.

 Read John 18:33–37. What statement of Jesus Christ confirms to us that He had been preparing for this moment His entire life on earth (v. 37)?

Please don't lose the significance of this statement: *"For this I have come into the world"* (v. 37). When considering the fact that Christ walked directly toward the Cross from the moment His tiny feet could steady Himself, we must see more in the crucifixion than the splintered wood and bloody ritual. Christ was purposeful in walking toward the only act that would ever redeem people and reconcile them to God. Every day of His life on earth was a testimony that He loved you and me and was willing to walk toward a cruel death in order that we could gain access to God through Him.

 Write a simple prayer expressing gratitude that Jesus remained faithful on this journey toward the reason He was born.

The crowd that day could not understand this truth. Pilate, realizing that he could find no charge against Jesus, went before the crowd and offered a compromise. He reminded them of a custom practiced at the time of Passover: the crowd was allowed to choose one prisoner to be set free, regardless of his crime.

"But you have a custom that I release someone for you at the Passover; do you wish then that I release for you the King of the Jews?" So they cried out again, saying, "Not this Man, but Barabbas." Now Barabbas was a robber.
—John 18:39–40

 Who did the crowd choose to be released that day (v. 40)?

Although Jesus Christ was not found guilty of any valid charge, He was held as a prisoner while a convicted robber was set free at the crowd's demand.

So we leave our Lord there with Pilate for the moment. The crowd of those who hated Him without due cause and desired nothing less than His life sacrificed on a cross would have that desire fulfilled. Yet many would be blind to the event that would take place right there before them.

Personal Reflection

1. **Have I ever misunderstood a situation in my life in which God was at work and I could not understand, so I took things into my own hands and performed wrongful actions (like Peter did when he cut off a person's ear in his effort to defend Christ)?**

2. **What tendencies do I have to deny Jesus Christ in exchange for perceived freedom to do other things?**

The Word in the World

Allison: Can You Suggest a Good Book on Religion?

As I walked past the nurses' station one day, I heard someone exclaim, "No crazy! Good Friday is the Friday before Easter."

"Oh," Allison replied. "I thought there were, like, a couple a year."

When they saw me, Allison asked if I could suggest any good books on religion for them to read.

I quickly said, "I know one *great* book!"

In unison they asked, "What, the Bible?" Then they continued their conversation.

That evening I purchased a Bible for Allison. I enclosed a letter that directed her to the exact pages where she could read the reports of the Crucifixion on Good Friday and the Resurrection.

The next day, I gave her the Bible. Tears came to her eyes as she told me thanks and said she would read it.

The Crucifixion Finishes the Work

People Introduced

Mary's sister (Jesus's aunt)

Mary (wife of Clopas)

Mary Magdalene (follower of Christ, who had cast seven demons from her; supporter of Christ with her substance and with her presence through His death and resurrection; first to whom the risen Christ appeared)

The disciple whom Jesus loved (traditionally believed to be John, author of this book)

Joseph of Arimathea (secretly a disciple of Christ; man of wealth; honorable member of the Sanhedrin [Jewish supreme judicial and administrative council]; one of the two men who buried Jesus)

> *Therefore when Jesus had received the sour wine, He said, "It is finished!" And He bowed His head and gave up His spirit.*
> —John 19:30

Are you already a little confused after looking at the list of people named Mary? I have wondered many times why God put so many Marys in the Scriptures. I know it was a common name for the period, but I think it would have been much easier had He incorporated some Veronicas or Susies in the mix just to break things up a bit.

Although some persons mentioned in the Scriptures share a name, each person included is unique and well worth us studying and understanding his or her relationship to Christ and individual role in God's plan. Some are given only a quick reference or cameo appearance; others reappear in several chapters. Each one is placed in the Scriptures to teach us a lesson. Let us dig into this week's study, ready to learn about some of the individuals present at the foot of the Cross and others who prepared Christ's lifeless body for the grave.

John 19:1–16

Last week's lesson ended with Jesus having been brought before the Roman governor, Pilate. Barabbas, a convicted felon, was set free, and Jesus Christ was held with no proof of guilt and was soon to face an increasingly angry crowd. Pilate, presumably trying to appease the bloodthirsty appetite of the masses, had Jesus scourged: *"Pilate then took Jesus and scourged Him"* (John 19:1).

 Without looking ahead, write your definition of *scourging*.

This scourging, or flogging, was no mere slap on the hand given mockingly to someone in hopes of deterring him or her from a future repetitive action. Flogging was a very painful and often public course of punishment that usually brought the person being flogged to the throes of death, and some victims probably would have rather chosen death over the experience. Typically, a scourging whip comprised several long strands of leather, each fashioned with fragments of bone or metal. When used in the hands of a person with experience, this tool of torture would quickly turn a bare back into a mess of mangled, raw flesh.

In further attempts to insult Christ, the soldiers placed a crown of thorns on His head and covered Him with a purple robe. Purple has historically been recognized as a symbol of royalty. Therefore, placing the crown of thorns and robe of purple on Christ was a way of mocking Christ's alleged role as king of the Jews.

 Discuss the symbolism of the crown and robe as compared with Jesus's statement in John 18:36–37.

> *Jesus answered, "My kingdom is not of this world. If My kingdom were of this world, then My servants would be fighting so that I would not be handed over to the Jews; but as it is, My kingdom is not of this realm." Therefore Pilate said to Him, "So You are a king?" Jesus answered, "You say correctly that I am a king. For this I have been born, and for this I have come into the world, to testify to the truth. Everyone who is of the truth hears My voice."*
> —John 18:36–37

Jesus Christ, the true King of kings (Revelation 19:16), was then stripped, beaten, and spit upon in open defiance by the very people He came to save. As a believer, it is tempting to feel intense anger for those Jews who did this to Him. I might even think such things as, *How dare they! Don't they know whom they are mocking?* Yet we must remember that apart from a personal, saving faith in Christ, we stand in their very shoes. Although we are not in a position to slap the physical face of Christ, defiance against proclaiming Him as Savior and Lord is just as stinging an insult.

Referring to John 3:16–18, write your answer to the following question: How does the disbelief of a person today place him or her in a similar stance of outright rebellion against Christ?

"For God so loved the world, that He gave His only begotten Son, that whoever believes in Him shall not perish, but have eternal life. For God did not send the Son into the world to judge the world, but that the world might be saved through Him. He who believes in Him is not judged; he who does not believe has been judged already, because he has not believed in the name of the only begotten Son of God."
—John 3:16–18

After having been flogged, Christ was brought before the crowd, robed in purple and with the crown of thorns on His head. Pilate declared, and not only once, *"I find no guilt in Him"* (John 19:4, 6). Yet the chief priests and officers cried out repeatedly: *"Crucify, crucify!"* (v. 6). Pilate then told the Jews to take Jesus away and crucify Him themselves.

Having been found not guilty under Roman law by Pilate, with what crime was Christ charged, according to the Jews?

The Jews answered him, "We have a law, and by that law He ought to die because He made Himself out to be the Son of God."
—John 19:7

The only crime that Jesus could rightly have been charged with was claiming to be God. According to the Jewish tradition, anyone who claimed to be God was charged with blasphemy and condemned to die. However, in this case, the One charged was speaking truth.

When Pilate heard this accusation, he was afraid. All of a sudden, bigger issues were at stake. Pilate asked Jesus, *"Where are You from?"* (John 19:9). If Christ had been a mere man, who enjoyed playing tricks on His fellow countrymen, this would have definitely been the time to come clean and save His hide! Instead, He stood by His declaration. Jesus made it clear that Pilate had no authority over Him except that which was given Pilate from above. After that, Pilate tried to release Jesus. But the Jews charged that Pilate was *"no friend of Caesar"* if he released Jesus (v. 12), so Pilate relented and handed Jesus Christ over to His countrymen to be crucified (v. 16).

John 19:17–24

Following the tradition of that time, Jesus was forced to carry His own cross down the streets, up the hill, and finally to the place where His burden would become the instrument of His death.

 What thoughts do you imagine were going through Christ's mind as He carried His cross to the place of His execution?

I am astounded when I consider the fact that at any point during this struggle, Christ could have said, "OK, this is enough; I am not doing this any longer." Had I been in His place, I definitely believe I would have taken an out. Thankfully, His love for His Father and us far exceeded any temporary anguish and pain He endured.

Upon arriving at the place called Golgotha, Jesus Christ was crucified. On His cross was placed a sign prepared by Pilate; it read, *"JESUS THE NAZARENE, THE KING OF THE JEWS"* (v. 19). Because of the multiethnic travel in the area, the sign was written in three languages: Hebrew, Latin, and Greek. The Jewish chief priests were less than thrilled at the wording and demanded that Pilate change the phrasing. Despite their arguments, the sign remained as written.

Read John 19:19–22. What is the significant difference between the wording Pilate had written on the sign and the phrase to which the Jewish priests wanted it to be changed?

Pilate also wrote an inscription and put it on the cross. It was written, "JESUS THE NAZARENE, THE KING OF THE JEWS." Therefore many of the Jews read this inscription, for the place where Jesus was crucified was near the city; and it was written in Hebrew, Latin and in Greek. So the chief priests of the Jews were saying to Pilate, "Do not write, 'The King of the Jews'; but that He said, 'I am King of the Jews.'" Pilate answered, "What I have written I have written."
—John 19:19–22

John 19:25–30

Mary, Jesus's mother, along with several others, stayed at the foot of Jesus's cross during the entire ordeal. Consider the fact that the mother who had borne and raised Jesus Christ was standing there watching His life slip away. Though she knew from the moment of His divine conception that He had a specific plan to fulfill, her mother's heart must have broken as she watched her child gasp for His final breaths. However, as we focus on Mary's concern for her son, we must not miss Jesus's concern for His mother, even at the climax of His own torture.

Describe the transfer of responsibility and care that occurred in John 19:26–27.

When Jesus then saw His mother, and the disciple whom He loved standing nearby, He said to His mother, "Woman, behold, your son!" Then He said to the disciple, "Behold, your mother!" From that hour the disciple took her into his own household.
—John 19:26–27

Shortly after the tender moment when Christ made arrangements for the care of His mother, He prepared to surrender Himself to death.

 Read John 19:30, and write out Christ's final three words.

Christ's statement, *"It is finished!"* (John 19:30) speaks of the totality and completion of the mission of Christ. He came to this earth for that moment. He allowed Himself to be captured and die upon the Cross. And it was through the spilling of His blood alone that a perfect, sinless sacrifice was made as a full atonement for all sin. Upon His death, it was finished. Our pathway to God was paved and wide open (Hebrews 10:19–20).

 Upon reviewing the verses below, write after each one your own understanding of what it says about the process of salvation.

For all have sinned and fall short of the glory of God.
—Romans 3:23

For the wages of sin is death, but the free gift of God is eternal life in Christ Jesus our Lord.
—Romans 6:23

But God demonstrates His own love toward us, in that while we were yet sinners, Christ died for us.
—Romans 5:8

If you confess with your mouth Jesus as Lord, and believe in your heart that God raised Him from the dead, you will be saved; for with the heart a person believes, resulting in righteousness, and with the mouth he confesses, resulting in salvation.
—Romans 10:9–10

Jesus said to him, "I am the way, and the truth, and the life; no one comes to the Father but through Me." [Explains the absolute necessity of faith in Jesus Christ alone]
—John 14:6

We do not find in the Scriptures any hint that we as humans must create our own path to God. Instead, we do find that all have sinned and that apart from faith in Jesus Christ, we are hopeless in our pursuit of the full life, hopeless in our search for God. When Christ's words, *"It is finished!"* were spoken, the path to God was completed. Christ was the plan all along.

John 19:31–42

Returning to the text regarding Christ's crucifixion, we see that Pilate granted permission for the legs of the men being crucified to be broken in order to hasten their deaths. When the soldiers came to Jesus and noticed He was already dead, they did not follow through with the act of breaking His bones and, instead, pierced His side with a sword. Therefore, not one bone of Jesus Christ was broken. This was meant to be, because it was fittingly prophesied years before His arrival on the earth.

Recall that in the beginning of John 19, we are told that Christ was crucified around the time of Passover. This event is a special religious celebration for the Jews because it reminds them that years before, God spared the lives of many of His people by instructing them to sacrifice a Passover lamb and spread the blood of the animal over their doorways and on the doorposts. Those who were faithful to this commandment had the lives of their firstborn spared from death. Those who chose to ignore the warning suffered death in their households. Yearly, Jews celebrate remembrance of this event by preparing a symbolic Passover meal, including a Passover lamb. However, specific rules must be followed when preparing and handling the body of the lamb.

Read the following verses to find some of the rules concerning the appropriate treatment of a Passover lamb. What one rule do you find in both passages?

"It is to be eaten in a single house; you are not to bring forth any of the flesh outside of the house, nor are you to break any bone of it."
—Exodus 12:46

"They shall leave none of it until morning, nor break a bone of it; according to all the statute of the Passover they shall observe it."
—Numbers 9:12

Although there were many specific rules regarding the Passover lamb, one that is found in both of these verses is that none of the animal's bones are to be broken. Though God chose to spare many of His people through the Passover event using a lamb and its blood, He later sent Jesus Christ to be the perfect and timeless sacrificial "Lamb" (John 1:29) who would die once and for all for our sins.

Using what you know about the treatment of the Passover lamb, how do the following verses demonstrate that Christ was regarded as our Perfect Lamb?

So the soldiers came, and broke the legs of the first man and of the other who was crucified with Him; but coming to Jesus, when they saw that He was already dead, they did not break His legs.
—John 19:32–33

For these things came to pass to fulfill the Scripture, "NOT A BONE OF HIM SHALL BE BROKEN."
—John 19:36

Pull Up a Chair

God had indeed saved His people *once* through their act of faith concerning a sacrificial lamb; however, on the day of Christ's crucifixion, He saved His people *forever* through a one-time act of sacrificing the Son, Jesus Christ. Therefore, He no longer demands acts of sacrifice to obtain salvation. Christ did that work on the Cross. The only requirement that is now necessary for salvation is that we place our faith in Him.

We will end this week's lesson by taking a glance at Christ's burial. Two men were involved in preparing His body for the tomb: Joseph of Arimathea and Nicodemus. Yes, Nicodemus is back in the picture, even though we have heard little about him since his visit with Jesus Christ one night, as recorded in John 3.

Joseph of Arimathea, secretly a disciple of Jesus Christ, asked Pilate for the body of Christ, and Nicodemus brought a mixture of spices to use in preparing the body for burial. The two of them wrapped Christ's body in linen cloths with aromatic spices. We are told little more about these burial hours, except that Christ's body was laid in a new tomb in a garden near where He had been crucified. However, we will soon discover in chapter 20 that His followers' time of weeping and mourning was cut dramatically short! Praise God!

Personal Reflection

1. **If I have a relationship with Christ, having walked through the verses that can help lead another to faith in Him, what (if any) are the reasons I am not currently sharing my faith?**

2. **If I have not placed my faith in Christ, what is blocking me from understanding the necessity of a personal relationship with Him?**

The Word in the World

Magda: Why Hasn't Anyone Told Me This?

When living in Poland, I sat on my couch with Magda, a new believer, and read through 1 Thessalonians. Magda had accepted Christ as Lord and Savior just four months earlier, and we were having our weekly time of discipleship.

When we read through the passages that speak of Christ's return, she suddenly jumped up and said, "Oh, my gosh. This is wonderful! Why hasn't anyone told me about this before?"

She then shared with me all the names of her family members and some others who did not have faith in Christ—all those with whom she wanted to share this good news soon so that they too could experience this newfound joy.

I sat there watching in awe the glow of faith on this new believer's face and thinking to myself, *Why haven't I told more people?*

> *Then the woman left her water jar, went into town, and told the men, "Come, see a man who told me everything I ever did! Could this be the Messiah?"*
> —John 4:28–29 (HCSB)

> *Mary Magdalene went and announced to the disciples, "I have seen the Lord!" And she told them what He had said to her.*
> —John 20:18 (HCSB)

Week 20   John 20

He Is Risen!

People Introduced
No new people introduced

Mary Magdalene came, announcing to the disciples, "I have seen the Lord," and that He had said these things to her.
—John 20:18

John 20:1–10
The Crucifixion and the Resurrection events are the foundations for our holidays known as Good Friday and Easter Sunday. Christ was crucified on *"the day of preparation for the Passover"* (John 19:14, see also vv. 31, 42), which most historians agree would have been a Friday. Then Mary Magdalene came to the tomb early *"on the first day of the week,"* saw that the stone had been moved away from the tomb's opening (v. 1), and became aware that Jesus's body was no longer in the tomb. The *"first day"* spoken about in verse 1 suggests Sunday, the actual first day of each week (unlike our typical Monday through Friday work week for which many consider Monday the first day). So Christ's body was noted to be missing on the third day from the time of His death, counting the day of His death as the first day and each partial day as one day (in Jewish thought).

 How does the timing of three days relate to the prophecy Jesus spoke in John 2:18–22?

The Jews then said to Him, "What sign do You show us as your authority for doing these things?" Jesus answered them, "Destroy this temple, and in three days I will raise it up." The Jews then said,

"It took forty-six years to build this temple, and will You raise it up in three days?" But He was speaking of the temple of His body. So when He was raised from the dead, His disciples remembered that He said this; and they believed the Scripture and the word which Jesus had spoken.
—John 2:18–22

It was early in the morning when Mary Magdalene arrived at the tomb, but she noticed the stone that had covered the opening had been moved away. The stones used to cover the tomb entrances were no small pebbles! Once rolled into place, those heavy stones were expected to stay there permanently. Therefore, the fact that the stone had been moved would definitely have been a surprise.

 According to John 20:2, what was Mary's immediate reaction when she saw the stone had been moved?

She immediately ran to some of the disciples. Can you blame her? Mary knew that her Lord had recently been buried in that tomb, and that the stone door had been sealed shut. Had I been there, I imagine Mary would have had company racing away from the site. Ordinary graveyards are eerie enough for me. How much more so would one be if something were obviously out of the ordinary? But we will ignore my personal graveyard hang-up and look at what crossed Mary's mind at her discovery.

So she ran and came to Simon Peter and to the other disciple whom Jesus loved, and said to them, "They have taken away the Lord out of the tomb, and we do not know where they have laid Him."
—John 20:2

 What does Mary's statement to Simon Peter and John (the disciple whom Jesus loved) reveal about her perception of the situation?

Pull Up a Chair

When the disciples arrived at the tomb, they found only the linen cloths, including the head wrapping, that Joseph of Arimathea and Nicodemus had carefully wrapped around Christ's dead body. Yet no body was found.

> *The two were running together; and the other disciple ran ahead faster than Peter and came to the tomb first; and stooping and looking in, he saw the linen wrappings lying there; but he did not go in. And so Simon Peter also came, following him, and entered the tomb; and he saw the linen wrappings lying there, and the face-cloth which had been on His head, not lying with the linen wrappings, but rolled up in a place by itself. So the other disciple who had first come to the tomb then also entered, and he saw and believed. For as yet they did not understand the Scripture, that He must rise again from the dead. So the disciples went away again to their own homes.*
> —John 20:4–10

 According to the preceding passage, what conclusion do you think the disciples made upon discovering the linens?

The disciples assessed the situation, then went away to their homes. They did not immediately realize that Christ had risen (v. 9). They had traveled and lived with Christ for years and heard all of His teachings, yet, standing in the midst of the resurrection room, even they did not understand all that Christ had tried to share with them. Let this remind us that the disciples were not extraordinary men with amazing faith and gifts; rather, they were *ordinary* men, much like you and me, with an *extraordinary* Savior. God used them greatly, and we are given the same promises and provisions today in Jesus Christ as they had.

John 20:11–18

The two disciples had returned to their homes, still in the dark as to what precisely had happened up to this point. Mary, however, hung around the site and was crying.

 What thoughts or emotions do you imagine Mary Magdalene might have experienced?

She apparently got braver, because she looked inside the tomb to see for herself that Jesus's body was gone. What she saw, however, was anything but an empty tomb!

 Describe the scene Mary witnessed inside Christ's tomb, as reported in John 20:12.

The Scripture states Mary saw two angels, but I wonder if she realized they were angels when she was talking with them. The conversation seems far too normal for me to assume she knew she was speaking to angelic beings. When the angels asked why she was crying, Mary simply told them, *"Because they have taken away my Lord, and I do not know where they have laid Him"* (John 20:13).

Next, she encountered the very One for whom she was weeping! Don't miss a single exciting detail about this first appearance of Christ after His resurrection.

 Read John 20:14–17 aloud, and answer the questions that follow.

When she had said this, she turned around and saw Jesus standing there, and did not know that it was Jesus. Jesus said to her, "Woman, why are you weeping? Whom are you seeking?" Supposing Him to be the gardener, she said to Him, "Sir, if you have carried Him away, tell me where you have laid Him, and I will take Him away." Jesus said to her, "Mary!" She turned and said to Him in Hebrew, "Rabboni!" (which means, Teacher). Jesus said to her, "Stop clinging to Me, for I have not yet ascended to the Father; but go to My brethren and say to them, 'I ascend to My Father and your Father, and My God and your God.'"
—John 20:14–17

- **Who did Mary initially think was speaking to her?**

- **Considering the fact that Mary thought the risen Christ was the gardener, what information does this give us about Jesus Christ's resurrected body?**

- **What did Jesus do that caused Mary to recognize Him?**

- **Write the commands Jesus Christ gave Mary.**

I love the closing remarks in Christ's command for Mary to go tell the others. Notice that He told her to go to His *"brethren,"* referring to His disciples, and say, *"I ascend to My Father and your Father, and My God and your God"* (John 20:17). As Christ's followers did the will of the Father—believed in *"Him whom He has sent"* (that is, came to faith in Christ [John 6:29; 1 John 3:23])—they were granted the right to call God the Father their very own Father and their God. Do you see this? As we become children of God through faith in Jesus Christ, the Creator God of the universe takes on a new role in our lives—the role of Father.

John 20:19–23

The next postresurrection event recorded in John 20 occurred the evening of that same day that the risen Christ was first seen. The disciples were gathered together behind closed doors. I'm sure there must have been some unrecorded rushed meetings at fellow disciples' homes saying such things as, "Have you heard? Mary has seen the Lord!" Yet any excitement they might have experienced upon first hearing the news had evaporated by this point because the fear of their fellow Jews had driven them to gather behind closed doors.

> *So when it was evening on that day, the first day of the week, and when the doors were shut where the disciples were, for fear of the Jews, Jesus came and stood in their midst and said to them, "Peace be with you."*
> —John 20:19

 What were Jesus's first words to His disciples (v. 19)?

In stark contrast to the immediate fear they were experiencing, Jesus appeared among them and announced, *"Peace be with you!"* (v. 19). Next, He showed them

His hands and side, and they rejoiced in realizing He was truly Jesus, their Lord—the One whom they had loved and served, the One who had been crucified. In the next few moments, Christ gave them an important commission: *"As the Father has sent Me, I also send you"* (John 20:21).

 Write your best understanding of this commission.

After saying these words, Christ breathed on His disciples and told them to receive the Holy Spirit—the Counselor, the Helper, the Comforter, who had been promised to them (John 14:16–17). Although Christ would soon be leaving again, the disciples were now to be permanently indwelt by God the Spirit.

John 20:24–31

Create this mental image with me: The disciples had been in the room and witnessed this amazing event—all except Thomas. When they all told him the grand story with gripping details and bone-chilling descriptions of Christ's appearance, Thomas was not buying it. Firmly he proclaimed, *"Unless I see in His hands the imprint of the nails, and put my finger into the place of the nails, and put my hand into His side, I will not believe"* (John 20:25).

 Have you ever felt like Thomas in your own faith? Please share a brief illustration.

Thomas's proclamation was no small act of doubt. Thomas listed three specific things he would have to experience before he would believe: see the mark of the nails, put his fingers into the nail marks, and put his hand in the wound in Jesus Christ's side. Do you find yourself frustrated with Thomas? You might be thinking, *Good grief! Everyone else saw Christ. Why couldn't Thomas just believe them?* Thankfully, God is much greater than our doubt.

Eight days later, Thomas was with the group of disciples, and Christ appeared in the midst of them once more.

We need to understand the variation and frequency of the postresurrection appearances of Christ. Many critics wish to summarize the Resurrection of Christ as a lie and the claims of witnesses as "mass hallucination." However, the Scriptures record not just one appearance but multiple appearances and to different people each time.

 Has the realization that Christ appeared more than once challenged your understanding of the Resurrection? If so, how?

Look carefully at the physical proof Christ provided to address the doubts of one of His disciples. Christ reappeared at a time when Thomas was with the other disciples. Rather than criticizing him for his doubts, Christ allowed him to fulfill his desires—Christ offered all Thomas's stated requirements for belief.

> *Then He said to Thomas, "Reach here with your finger, and see My hands; and reach here your hand and put it into My side; and do not be unbelieving, but believing."*
> —John 20:27

 How do you imagine Thomas must have felt the moment he was permitted to place his hands in the wounds of his Lord's hands and side and put his doubts to rest?

The emotive side of me always swells up when I read this passage. I think, *Wow, it must have been amazing to see our resurrected Savior and to be allowed to actually touch Him and to know from this that everything was all right.* And though you may share the same desire, Christ spoke directly to those of us who must walk by faith.

> *Jesus said to him, "Because you have seen Me, have you believed? Blessed are they who did not see, and yet believed."*
> —John 20:29

What promise is given to those of us who believe by faith alone?

Christ is aware of our tendencies to doubt at times. Yet He reminds us that it is more blessed to believe by faith than by sight. In times when our faith seems shallow, we can rest assured that our clearest faith vision is found through the study of God's Word. In His Word, we find our Source of strength and endurance, our faith food.

John admitted that Jesus performed in the presence of His disciples many other signs that were not written down. However, those signs that were recorded by John were included for one specific purpose.

According to the following verse, what was John's specific purpose for recording what he did?

But these have been written so that you may believe that Jesus is the Christ, the Son of God; and that believing you may have life in His name.
—John 20:31

The life, ministry, death, and Resurrection of Jesus Christ were all for one purpose: *"that you may believe that Jesus is the Christ, the Son of God; and that believing you may have life in His name"* (John 20:31). It is only through this belief and confession that we are freed from the bondage of sin and allowed to walk in grace. Personal belief about Christ Jesus is the crux of everything else we do in life. It will determine our morality, our livelihood, our hope, and our eternal direction. Who do you believe that Jesus is?

Personal Reflection

1. Does my life reflect the belief that I am serving an alive and risen Savior, or do my actions align more with the concept of Christ still being in His tomb?

2. If I know Christ, am I living in the peace that He immediately offered His disciples upon His return?

3. If I do not know Christ, is there a part of me that desires that peace with Him?

The Word in the World

Ally: The Reapers Rejoice

One afternoon I found myself rejoicing with the reapers.

My husband and I had recently cleaned up the sand volleyball court in our backyard and were using it with the youth group for outreach purposes. While sitting on the sidelines during a game, I noticed a young girl approach the court on a bike. I walked over to her and introduced myself.

"Hi," she responded. "My name is Ally. I just thought I would stop by to check you guys out."

As Ally and I sat together on the sidelines, I began to ask her questions. She told me that she had just returned home from a church camp, which she had attended with a relative. The good news was that, while at camp, she had accepted Christ as her Savior!

She then said, "I now realize that I need to be involved in a youth group, and when I saw you guys outside, I thought I would come over and check things out."

I had the joy of hearing Ally's testimony and then talking with her about baptism. Within two months, my husband baptized her, and she is now a vital part of our youth ministry. God dropped Ally into our hands. We were not there to sow the seed of truth in her life; we were just blessed to reap the harvest of what another planted.

> *"For in this case the saying is true, 'One sows and another reaps.'*
> *I sent you to reap that for which you have not labored; others have*
> *labored and you have entered into their labor."*
> —John 4:37–38

Risen Jesus Appears Again

Jesus said to them, "Come and have breakfast." None of the disciples ventured to question Him, "Who are You?" knowing that it was the Lord. Jesus came and took the bread and gave it to them, and the fish likewise. This is now the third time that Jesus was manifested to the disciples, after He was raised from the dead.
—John 21:12–14

Endings and New Beginnings

As we begin our study of this last chapter of John, I want to share a few words about endings and beginnings. Endings have always been a source of bittersweet emotion for me. I pounce on new experiences with unbridled joy and walk away from completed journeys with a mixture of wonderful memories and often unshed tears. I pray that as we have journeyed together through this part of God's Word, you have not only created memories with one another but also experienced precious times of treasure with your Creator. Hold fast to what you have gleaned from the Scriptures, and let this study be a stepping-stone toward a longer, more in-depth exploration into the Word of God. As we wind up this week, be praying about which book the Lord wants you to dive into next. The Bible contains countless treasures that are yours for the taking if only you know the Primary Author and diligently search His Word.

John 21:1–14

After having seen the risen Christ on two prior occasions, the disciples gained back much of their courage. They were no longer cowering behind closed doors but were out on the sea performing typical work for this period. Fishing was not only a means for many to make money; it was also a typical means to ensure food was on the family table! Therefore, the scene of men in a boat was as common then as the scene of men wearing suits and walking into an office building is today. So it was on this ordinary day, in these ordinary circumstances, that Christ decided to make another appearance to His disciples (His third group appearance, according to the Gospel of John).

 According to John 21:4, at what time of the day did Jesus appear on the shoreline?

The risen Lord came to His disciples again one morning at daybreak. The disciples did not immediately recognize the Man who spoke to them from the shoreline as being Jesus. Early morning fog or lack of a fully risen sun may have hindered their vision, but other factors were likely involved in this lack of recognition as well (see Luke 24:15–16, 30–31). Their "vision," however, cleared up after Jesus spoke and things happened. The disciples recognized Him not only through His voice but also through his actions and authority.

 Do you see any correlation between the time that Mary Magdalene first recognized the risen Christ when He spoke her name (John 20:15–16) and the time the disciples recognized the shoreline figure as Christ (John 21:5–7)?

Jesus said to her, "Woman, why are you weeping? Whom are you seeking?" Supposing Him to be the gardener, she said to Him, "Sir, if you have carried Him away, tell me where you have laid Him, and I will take Him away." Jesus said to her, "Mary!" She turned and said to Him in Hebrew, "Rabboni!" (which means, Teacher).
—John 20:15–16

So Jesus said to them, "Children, you do not have any fish, do you?" They answered Him, "No." And He said to them, "Cast the net on the right-hand side of the boat and you will find a catch." So they cast, and then they were not able to haul it in because of the great number of fish. Therefore that disciple whom Jesus loved said to Peter, "It is the Lord." So when Simon Peter heard that it was the

Lord, he put his outer garment on (for he was stripped for work), and threw himself into the sea.
—John 21:5–7

Now, referring to John 10:3–5, how would you explain to a new believer the importance of hearing and knowing God's voice?

"To him the doorkeeper opens, and the sheep hear his voice, and he calls his own sheep by name and leads them out. When he puts forth all his own, he goes ahead of them, and the sheep follow him because they know his voice. A stranger they simply will not follow, but will flee from him, because they do not know the voice of strangers."
—John 10:3–5

The voice of God has not been muted or muffled over the years. As believers today, we also have opportunity to hear Him and recognize His voice and activity. He speaks to us regularly through the living Scriptures, the Word of God. The pages contain His promises and teachings. By faith, we must accept that the Lord has protected His Word through time and allowed His message to arrive to us today intact and infallible.

Write a statement describing the relationship between recognizing God's voice and the study of the Scriptures.

Upon recognizing Christ, Peter made a radical decision to leave the comfort of the boat and dive into the sea to get to his Lord quicker. Abandoning all, Peter demonstrated his urgent desire to be with Christ.

Where on the following line would you rate your current desire to know and obey Christ?

↑	↑	↑
I am still in the comfort of my "boat."	**I am willing to step out of my comfort zone.**	**I am already deep in the water, following Christ.**

Knowing where you are is the first step in making a true decision in following Christ.

Now let us take a closer look at the Christ we are to follow and the hope we have in Him. The Christ presented in the Scriptures is the God of all creation who was born in the flesh and willingly and lovingly gave His life for our sin. He died a cruel death, left a tomb empty (other than linen cloths) after His resurrection, and appeared on various occasions to His followers. The Resurrection of Christ from death back to life was just as essential to our salvation as was His death on the Cross. Had Christ died, been buried, and remained forever in the tomb, our hope would have been sealed within the grave with Him. The fact that He suffered and experienced and ultimately escaped the grip of death has paved the way for us to escape death too! He conquered the finality of death. We who have placed our faith in Christ are no longer subject to the power and authority of death. Though our earthly bodies will someday give way to decline, our souls will escape the termination of death (John 11:25–26) and live eternally in His presence. This one fact is cause enough for us to rejoice daily. Yet it is also cause enough for each of us to stop and consider our own path. If we have not individually made the decision to accept Christ as Savior, the consequences of death are still a part of our future.

 Have you ever truly faced the reality of your future apart from a relationship with Jesus Christ?

 On what or whom are you basing your hope for eternal life?

My deepest prayer for you is that you can honestly say, "Yes, I have considered the reality that my sin has separated me from God, and I have placed my faith in Jesus Christ as my Lord and Savior, my only hope for eternal life." Though those exact words hold no magical power, they express the reality of what the Scriptures have taught us. Every one of us has sinned (Romans 3:23). The result of our sin is death (Romans 6:23). Placing our faith in the risen Christ, confessing Him as Lord, is our only opportunity to escape the eternal death rightfully due us (Romans 10:9–10).

John 21:15–19

In this next passage, Jesus Christ gave Peter the opportunity to confess his allegiance to Him three times. Three times was an appropriate number of times because, as we saw in chapter 18, Peter had denied Christ on three occasions. In these moments of Peter's reaffirmation recorded in John 21, Peter was allowed to confirm his declaration of love for Christ and experience restoration of their relationship.

> So when they had finished breakfast, Jesus said to Simon Peter, "Simon, son of John, do you love Me more than these?" He said to Him, "Yes, Lord; You know that I love You." He said to him, "Tend My lambs." He said to him again a second time, "Simon, son of John, do you love Me?" He said to Him, "Yes, Lord; You know that I love You." He said to him, "Shepherd My sheep." He said to him the third time, "Simon, son of John, do you love Me?" Peter was grieved because He said to him the third time, "Do you love Me?" And he said to Him, "Lord, You know all things; You know that I love You." Jesus said to him, "Tend My sheep."
> —John 21:15–17

 As Peter confessed his love for Jesus, what were the three commands Christ gave him?

An important way that we demonstrate our love for Christ is through the "feeding" and "shepherding" of His "sheep." We learned from John 10 that Christ referred to His followers as His sheep. Therefore, through our caring for, guiding, and protecting other Christ followers, we display our own commitment to Christ.

John 21:20–25

I cringe each time I read this next passage because I hear my own voice asking Peter's question, *"Lord, and what about this man?"* (John 21:21). I am often guilty of wanting to know more about what God is doing with others than what needs examining in my own life. Though Christ's answer may not sound overly harsh, do not miss the rebuke in His warning: *"If I want him to remain until I come, what is that to you? You follow Me!"* (John 21:22).

Summarize Jesus's response to Peter's question (vv. 22–23).

My summary is this: God is going to do what He wants to do in the lives of His people. Our primary role is to be first and foremost concerned about how we fit into His overall plan and stop worrying about what parts other people are playing in His masterpiece.

Can you relate to Peter's question? Have you ever lost your focus on God's plan for your own life and worried more about roles other people seemed to be playing? Please share an example in light detail.

The concluding verses in this chapter testify that John (the disciple whom Jesus loved) authored this particular Gospel. I love the closing words: *"We know that his testimony is true"* (John 21:24). The author of the Gospel of John walked with Christ during His earthly ministry, stood at the foot of the Cross during His death, assumed responsibility for our Lord Jesus Christ's mother, experienced the risen Christ, and wrote these accounts so that we, today, can know and believe.

Although John recorded only a few accounts of Christ's miracles during His ministry and only four postresurrection appearances (one to Mary, three to His disciples), we are told that Jesus did many other things, which, out of God's choosing and possibly for the sake of space, were not recorded.

And there are also many other things which Jesus did, which if they were written in detail, I suppose that even the world itself would not contain the books that would be written.
—John 21:25

How did John describe the enormity of the events that took place during Jesus's ministry?

Out of the multitude of conversations, walks, miracles, and other fantastic events that occurred during the life of Christ, those recorded in this book were recorded specifically for us to read and understand so that we may *"believe that Jesus is the Christ, the Son of God,"* and, believing thus, have life in His name (John 20:31). I challenge you to focus primarily not on what God chose *not* to include but rather on the information that He purposefully included in the Scriptures. Every detail, every word, was divinely chosen to land in our hands today. These words convict us of sin, reveal our need for a Savior, and deliver hope that can never fail. Savor them!

Personal Reflection

1. **How does my understanding of Christ compare with the truths taught about Him in the Scriptures?**

2. **What areas of my life have been challenged the most through the study of this book?**

3. Am I confident that I have a personal relationship with Jesus Christ and know how to hear His voice? (If your answer is no and you desire to have confirmation in these areas, please share your answer with a trusted Christian.)

4. Has the Lord challenged me in my ability to lead another woman through the study of His Word? If so, how?

5. Whom should I begin praying for in preparation for walking her or them through the Gospel of John?

Pass the Torch

Now that we have journeyed through the Gospel of John together (with some sweet fellowship along the way), the torch is yours to carry. I challenge you to prayerfully seek the Lord and identify a woman in your life with whom you may enter this journey as teacher and guide. May you be given the joy and privilege of seeing other women come to know Christ personally, one by one, through faith and knowledge of His Word.

Continue to search the Scriptures for God's truths. God's Word is your shield and firm foundation and can come to be the same for anyone who learns to love the Word. So share God's Word in your daily encounters with others. As you step out in faith, sharing God's Word and love, place your life and the results in God's hands.

My closing prayer for you is that you may forever find your life, peace, joy, and rest in God and in His Word.

New Hope® Publishers is a division of WMU®,
an international organization that challenges Christian believers
to understand and be radically involved in God's mission.
For more information about WMU, go to www.wmu.com.
More information about New Hope books may be found
at www.newhopepublishers.com. New Hope books
may be purchased at your local bookstore.

Books & Studies
to Equip You

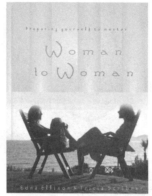

Woman to Woman
Preparing Yourself to Mentor
Edna Ellison and Tricia Scribner
ISBN-10: 1-56309-949-7
ISBN-13: 978-1-56309-949-6

Splash the Living Water
Sharing Jesus in Everyday Moments
Esther Burroughs
ISBN-10: 1-59669-002-X
ISBN-13: 978-1-59669-002-8

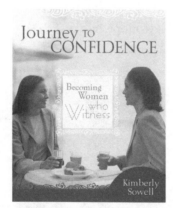

Journey to Confidence
Becoming Women Who Witness
Kimberly Sowell
ISBN-10: 1-56309-923-3
ISBN-13: 978-1-56309-923-6

Available in bookstores everywhere

For information about these books or any New Hope® product, visit www.newhopepublishers.com.